POINTING THE YOUNG TO CHRIST

Original Bible Object and
Flannelgraph Lessons

Written and Illustrated by
G. A. NEILSON

LONDON
PICKERING & INGLIS LTD.
1957

PICKERING & INGLIS LTD.

29 LUDGATE HILL, LONDON, E.C.4

229 BOTHWELL STREET, GLASGOW, C.2

Fleming H. Revell Company, 316 Third Avenue, Westwood, New Jersey

Home Evangel, 1 Waterman Avenue, Toronto, 16

Made and Printed in Great Britain

CONTENTS

Four Wonderful Birds

UNDER the blue Syrian sky, upon a green mound on the hillside, Jesus sat above the crowd which had gathered to hear His gracious words. During His preaching, He seems to have observed some birds as they flew overhead, for He said, "Behold the fowls of the air". Possibly He may have drawn attention to them also before proceeding to use them as an object lesson, in order to teach the important truth of simple trust in God. Here, likewise, are a few birds from which we, too, may learn some helpful lessons:—

A Bird of Prey (Job 39. 26). An American boy named  Jack Phillips shot and wounded a hawk. He thought he could tame it, so took it home and placed it in a barn beside his pet rabbits and pigeons. For a little while all went well, then one day, to his great dismay, Jack discovered that the hawk had killed nearly all his pets. Only then did he obey the previous instruction of his father by destroying it. Surely a costly pet! What a picture of sin we see in this fierce bird, the nature of which cannot be changed or improved, and which works such havoc and destruction on its victims. Sin, too, is far too strong for us; but we have in Christ a sure Protector and Saviour, to whom we may flee for refuge.

5

A Bird of Peace (Gen. 8. 12).   Suppose we imagine our-selves as being with Noah and his family inside the ark after the terrible deluge. The rain has long ceased, and the waters are disappearing rapidly.   The raven has been released, but has not been seen again. The dove, however, has just returned for the second time, bearing in its beak an olive leaf.   This bird brings great cheer to our hearts, for now we know that the waters of judgment have gone.   In a little while we'll be able to leave our place of refuge and go forth to enjoy a new life, in a new world, without any fears of another judgment.   Peace fills our hearts, therefore, and we sing for joy at this wonderful news brought to us by the dove.

This is a beautiful illustration of what happens when we believe God's message of warning and take refuge in Christ, our Ark of Refuge, from the coming judgment.   To us there comes the bird of peace bearing the joyful and assuring tidings that judgment has passed, for Jesus on the Cross bore it all. Now we have life everlasting and can never come into judgment (John 5. 24); so, every fear is dispelled, while peace and joy fill our hearts.

A Bird of Passage (Jer. 8. 7).   Let us suppose that it isearly summer.   We gaze heavenwards and see some swallows, with their beauti-ful plumage of glossy bluish-black, skim-ming through the air.   As we look closely at these birds, we begin to ask ourselves a few questions which have long puzzled the wisest of men—'How does the swallow know the exact time of year to migrate from one country to another?   Who gives it such wisdom?   How is it that this little bundle of feathers, weighing only a few ounces, can fly thousands of miles?' These are secrets which only God and the swallow know; but, the fact remains, that, as the season comes round, *it knows just* *when to fly away* to its new home in another country. It is this fact which God's Word emphasises in order to teach an important lesson, namely, that, *when God calls, we should respond immediately.*

A young girl lay very ill in hospital whom I was asked to visit. It was not a visiting day, so I was only allowed ten minutes with her. She had lain for several weeks without a visit from any Christian worker; but, when I told her of God's great love and Christ's death for her, she responded immediately by putting out her thin white hand and telling me that she wanted to trust the Saviour. Within a few days she passed away; but not before she had witnessed for her Lord and had asked one of the other girl patients to sing the hymn, 'I know that my Redeemer liveth'. Anna was just like the swallow, for she knew the time of her opportunity and grasped it at once.

What a courageous little bird is the swallow, also, for *it refuses to be kept back at migration time* from any fear of danger, distance, or difficulty which it might encounter on its long flight. It would seem to say to any who is timid about trusting Christ, "Don't be afraid, or worried, over the dangers of the flight to the New Country; for God will surely guide and protect you all along the way until you reach that happy sunny Land of Glory; so, *dare to follow where He leads!*"

A Bird of Paradise. The reason this bird gets its name is easy to understand for it excels all other birds in its magnificent plumes and glory of colour. It comes from the Malay Archipelago, and other adjoining countries in that part of the world, including, also, parts of Australia. One remarkable feature about it is that it is the male bird which is so colourful, while the female bird is relatively plain. Among the most striking forms are: the *Great Bird of Paradise*, the *King Paradise Bird*, with its glossy scarlet and bright green throat patch, and the *Magni-*

ficent Bird of Paradise with its wonderful ruff. Some of them have a sweeping mass of lovely feathers which fall over the tail like a sparkling waterfall of many colours. This beautiful bird with its vivid colours looks as though it has come from the Paradise above! It is certainly true to its name, for it makes us think of Heaven itself.

Although it is not named in Scripture, the Bird of Paradise reminds us of the references therein to Paradise, or Heaven. It is remarkable that, when Jesus died, He spoke of Paradise to the repentant thief beside Him and assured him with these precious words of comfort: 'Today shalt thou be with Me in Paradise' (Luke 23. 43). After the Fall, our first parents were expelled from the earthly Paradise and forbidden to re-enter it. When Jesus died, however, He opened the gates of a far better Paradise, the Heavenly one, not to innocent people, as in Eden, but to all those who, like the repentant thief, would trust Him as Saviour. As we look at this lovely bird, then, with its magnificent plumage, we think of the Happy Land above, which we may all enjoy at last if we open our hearts to the Saviour and bid Him enter in.

Thus we may learn many interesting and valuable truths from these four birds. The first one, the *hawk*, reminds us of our sinful nature and, therefore, our need of a new nature as taught by the Lord Jesus to Nicodemus (John 3. 7). The second bird, the *dove*, tells out the wonderful truth that there is salvation in Christ our Ark and that we should be His messengers of the glad tidings of salvation. The third bird, the *swallow*, reminds us that we should decide for Christ without delay (2 Cor. 6. 2). The last bird, the *bird of Paradise*, points forward to the heavenly home for all who trust the Saviour.

May we heed the words of the Lord Jesus, therefore, and "behold the birds", then thank Him for these four wonderful little preachers.

HATS to WEAR!

HERE are a number of hats which belong to different kinds of people in different walks of life, each with its own particular story to tell:—

The Straw Hat. A glance at this hat shows that its owner  lives in a warm country, possibly near the tropics. Inside the hat is a card which bears the word '*Sunshine*'; while, on the opposite side of it is the text, 'God is love' (1 John 4. 8). The message it conveys is this—*Live in the sunshine of the love of God.*

A gentleman who resided in Northern Ontario, where the temperature often drops to 50 degrees and more below zero during the coldest periods of winter, took seriously ill. His doctor advised him to remove to a warm climate immediately in order to save his life; so, within forty-eight hours, the sick man was flown to U.S.A. and from there to the West Indies. It was a tremendous change for him to come straight from the frozen north right into the warmth of the tropics; but it was the means, however, of restoring his health and saving his life.

There are many others, similarly, perishing in the cold of unbelief, who, if they would but come into the warmth of God's love, would be saved with His wonderful salvation, and enjoy a countless stream of blessings because of His great love.

The 'Mountie's' Hat. This large hat, with its broad brim,  is easily recognized as belonging to one of Canada's Mounted Police, so well known for their daring exploits. The card inside bears the word '*Guilt*'; while the text is Num. 32. 23, 'Be sure your sin will find you out.'

The work of the Mounted Police is to maintain law and order, particularly in the more remote parts of Canada. A message may be flashed to them from Police Headquarters concerning a 'wanted' person, who is known to have entered their district. We can imagine the follow up, and then the capture, with all its excitement, and finally, the judgment passed on the guilty person.

One lesson, among many others, which this hat would teach is, that *all sin will be found out*. How much better it is to confess one's sin now, and know the joy of God's forgiveness (1 John 1. 9), rather than, like Achan, to wait until the sin be exposed and judgment passed.

The Fireman's Hat. Whenever we see this hat we think of *danger* and perhaps picture someone trapped in a blazing building. What fire may do to life and property sin may do to body and soul. It may trap us and ruin us. Surely it teaches our need of a Saviour and our helplessness to save ourselves. But this hat has a message of *hope* and *cheer* as well. It tells us that a deliverer is at hand to rescue the perishing. He is quickly on the spot whenever he is called and, no matter how dangerous the work, he is ready to deliver. What a relief it must be when a person, cut off in a fire and too scared to jump from the window, sees the fireman appearing! Within a few minutes he hacks his way through and effects a timely rescue. And is that not a picture of what the Saviour is doing for all who, realising their danger, call upon Him? Thus we see that this hat reminds us of our danger and also that Christ is ready and able to save all who call upon Him (Rom. 10. 13).

The Chef's Hat. If we were permitted to visit the kitchen of a large hotel, we would probably be introduced to the gentleman who wears this large white hat. He is the person responsible for all the cooking arrangements so that everyone in the hotel may enjoy excellent meals. If we are allowed this visit, however, we would prefer to arrange it as near to Christmas as possible! The card inside the hat bears the word '*Feast*', with this text, 'Come, for all things are now ready' (Matt. 22. 4). It is the call to share in the Gospel Feast and partake of God's wonderful provision. As Joseph invited his guilty brothers to partake of his feast; or, as King David invited Mephibosheth to eat at his table continually; or, as the father of the Prodigal Son invited him to partake of his bounty at the special feast; so, likewise, we are all invited to eat at the King's Table and partake of the Gospel Banquet.

The Soldier's Hat. There are various kinds of headwear  for the modern soldier, of which this is one of the most popular. We can picture the young recruit, as he goes to the Quartermaster's store, where he is issued with his uniform and full kit, which includes this beret. When he enlisted in the Army, he swore allegiance to his Queen, and promised thereby to obey the orders of Her Majesty and all commanding officers. It is not surprising, then, that the card, in this case, should bear the word, 'Obedience'; while Matt. 8. 9 is the accompanying text, 'Do this and he doeth it.' By means of the uniform, the young man confesses that he is no longer a civilian, but a soldier of the Queen. Likewise, when anyone accepts Christ as Saviour and Lord, His Word enjoins that there should be a public confession of Christ by the young believer; or, in other words, that he should 'don the uniform.'

A young man met his Bible Class leader one Sunday evening and the conversation turned to this important subject of open confession of Christ. The lad was timid regarding this matter and made the suggestion: "Could I not be a Christian without telling my pals?" After being rebuked for his cowardice, he was shown from Romans 10. 9 that faith and confession must go together. After a few moments thought, the lad stretched out his hand in token of his willingness to make a public confession of Christ, and thus show his colours. Then they gripped each other's hand, and thus the King's uniform was donned!

The Miner's Hat. What an indispensable man is the miner! and what a necessary thing is his hat; for, not only does it protect his head, but it also carries the safety lamp, without which he could not work. His is a life of constant self-sacrifice, for he works under difficult circumstances, where the sun can never shine; where there are constant dangers to be faced and many hardships to be endured in order that homes and factories may be supplied with this precious mineral. Inside this hat is a card bearing the word, '*Work*,' while the text is, 'I must work the works of Him that sent Me' (John 9. 4). Just as the Saviour had to leave the glory of heaven, and descend into this dark world in order to reach and save us; so, likewise, His servants must be prepared to humble themselves and make sacrifice so that others may be brought 'out of darkness into His marvellous light' (1 Peter 2. 9). That is why we must carry the Light with us everywhere we go.

The Captain's Hat. This hat belongs to the Captain who is in charge of the ship, and is responsible for the safety of all who sail with him. He must possess his captain's certificate, and have a thorough knowledge of navigation. But that does not mean, however, that the passengers will never be sea-sick!

It means, rather, that no matter how many storms may be encountered, he will bring his vessel safely to port, and that is what our Captain (Heb. 2. 10) will do for all who trust Him. The word on the card, is '*Kept*', while the text is from 1 Peter 1. 5, 'Who are *kept* by the power of God.'

During a severe storm at sea, a ship was badly battered by a terrific gale and mountainous seas so that many of the passengers were on the verge of panic. Just then a little girl appeared among them, smiling, and apparently without any fear. When questioned as to the secret of her peace she just pointed in the direction of the bridge and exclaimed: "My daddy is the Captain, and he's up there." Though there may be many a storm on the sea of life, the believer also can look up and trust the Divine Captain to bring His vessel safely through every difficulty with all those who sail with Him.

Vans

OUR streets are filled with all sorts of trucks, vans, cars, etc., and it is an interesting sight watching them all juggling through the maze of traffic. Many of them are brightly coloured; while others are painted in more sombre shades. Whatever their colours may be, however, we can generally tell at a distance what kind of vehicles they are—and possibly, also, their particular make and names. Well, here is the first:—

The Police Van—'Black Maria' it is sometimes called and, as we can imagine, it is for prisoners, or those suspected of crime. Perhaps some thieves have been caught and, in answer to a police call, this Police Patrol Van is sent along. It has special wireless equipment also by means of which very urgent messages may be received from Police Hadquarters while the van is travelling, thus saving much valuable time.

If there were no sin in the world, this van would be unnecessary; but, as we know, that is not the case, and therefore it is in constant use. We can see the guilty look on the faces of the handcuffed men who are placed inside, with the probability of a long prison sentence before them. Across the van we may write these words in large letters—'All the world guilty before God' (Rom. 3. 19).

The Ambulance Van. This is, perhaps, the most useful vehicle of all, because of its sole purpose, namely, to rush sick or injured people to hospital, or bring them home again. By means of it much valuable time is saved, and precious lives likewise.

Sin is like a disease which may spread rapidly and end fatally. That is why we require the services of the Great Physician without delay, and also of those who would seek to bring the sin-sick ones to Him.

A friend of the writer, who was employed at a large steelworks, took seriously ill, and had to be rushed to hospital without delay. There were two hospitals available, but one was several miles further than the other. When the patient was recovering he remarked: 'If I had been taken to the other hospital it would probably have been too late.'

The Bread Van. In some places the baker may use a

whistle, or he may just shout 'Baker!' It is interesting to observe how children run towards him to see what he has for them in the way of tarts, cakes, and other dainties.

Across this van is the text, 'I am the Bread of Life: he that cometh to Me shall never hunger' (John 6. 35). Just as Jesus multiplied the five loaves and two fishes to feed the multitude in the desert; so, by giving Himself to die for us on the Cross, He has become the Bread of Life to all who accept Him. When we eat, we make the food our very own; likewise, when we believe, we make Christ our own and, by so doing, enjoy life everlasting. (Reference might also be made here to the School-Meals Van in its splendid work.)

The Laundry Van. This van may be seen very frequently as it has a never-ending job to do. It is so easy to get our

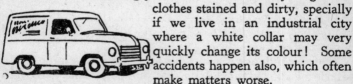

clothes stained and dirty, specially if we live in an industrial city where a white collar may very quickly change its colour! Some accidents happen also, which often make matters worse.

A lady in Manchester was standing at a bus stop, ready to board a bus, when, all of a sudden, her fine coat was blown against a lamp standard which had just been painted! An ugly streak of green paint stained the coat and ruined it.

Suppose we follow the soiled clothes to the laundry and watch them being cleaned. They are placed in huge cylinders which are then filled with soapy suds and boiling water. They are soaked, rubbed, and placed in a revolving machine; while the steam forces itself and the soap suds through and through the clothes until all stains and dirt are removed. Then follows the drying process and ironing, until they are ready to be parcelled for the van-man to deliver.

This is but an illustration of all who desire to get rid of the stains and defilement of sin, and be made 'whiter than the snow' through the cleansing blood of Christ (1 John 1. 7).

The Mail Van. The bright red colour enables us to spot this van easily and we read on it the words, 'Royal Mail.'

This is the van which brings letters from friends far and near, parcels, too, and good things—especially on birthdays, or at Christmas time!

The Gospel is indeed Good News. The Chinaman sometimes calls it 'the Good News from a Happy God.' Every Sunday School teacher, or preacher, is just like the mail man with his van, for they are bearers of good tidings of God's love and a Saviour's death so that sinners might be saved. The parcels also tell of the many gifts which God's wonderful love has provided, such as pardon, deliverance, life everlasting, sonship, peace, power, joy, the sure prospect of heaven, etc.

The Removal Van. Here is a family which has been living in a condemned dwelling for years because of the acute shortage of houses. It was both damp and dreary, for the sun never shone into a single room. No wonder there was constant sickness. Well, it is all changed now, for a new house has been provided and this is the removal day! The removal men are on the job and have the whole responsibility of removing everything, and also of laying linoleum, carpets, etc., in the new house.

It is another modern parable. The condemned house is the place where the unsaved one lives (John 3. 18), where there is no light, no joy, and no peace of mind. When we receive the Saviour, however, the removal takes place from 'Dismal Hovel' to 'Sunshine Villa!'

Boys! Boys!

HOW very many jobs a boy may do! No wonder, then, that we often see these familiar words in a shop window: 'SMART BOY WANTED,' for there never seems to be a sufficient number of these useful lads to satisfy all the demands! We're going to look at a few of these busy boys, therefore, and try to learn something from them:—

The News Boy or, *Something We Must Hear*. See him as he dashes along the street, shouting some important news

item, which brings crowds of customers around him. People are always interested in news, specially if it concerns themselves. Well, here is news which concerns every one of us—'*All* we like sheep have gone astray' (Isa. 53. 6); or, 'For *all* have sinned and come short of the glory of God' (Rom. 3. 23). Then, having learned of our need and danger, we are ready to listen to the next important news item—'For God so loved the *world* . . .' (John 3. 16). It seems almost too good to be true, that God should so love us as to give His only Son to save us; but we discover that it is indeed gloriously true.

The Baker's Boy or, *A Food We Must Eat*. He does his work well for he is at the door with regular punctuality, de-

livering morning rolls, bread, etc. From house to house he goes, until his task is completed; then he returns with his empty basket, happy to think that he has helped to provide essential food for not a few. As we look at this boy and his bread, we remember the familiar text, 'I am the bread of life: he that

16

cometh to Me shall never hunger . . .' (John 6. 35). We remember, too, the boy who gave his five barley loaves to Jesus and so helped to feed the multitude.

During the seige of Londonderry in 1690, the city refused to acknowledge James II, for they knew that he would deprive them of their religious liberties. For 105 days the terrible seige lasted, during which time the people quickly exhausted their food supplies and were compelled to live on rats, mice, etc., in order to keep themselves alive. At long last, however, the English fleet was sighted coming to their help. The ships burst through the boom and, at 10 p.m. that evening, a plentiful supply of food was distributed to every one of the famished citizens. Likewise, the Bread of Life is offered freely to us as perishing sinners, without money or price; but it must be accepted and eaten before we can be saved from perishing and thus enjoy Divine life.

The Telegram Boy or, *A Decision We Must Make*. This lad delivers a telegram to us and waits for a reply as requested,

so we must come to a decision at once. The matter is most urgent, and any delay on our part may be dangerous. Perhaps the telegram tells of the serious illness of a near relative who desires to see us; or, it may be the offer of an important position which must be filled at once. The decision, therefore, may influence our whole after-life, either for good or bad; therefore, it must be pondered thoughtfully. Then, having made up our minds as to the proper course to take, we write the reply wire and hand it to the lad. As he cycles back to the post office whistling as he goes, little does he realise that he is carrying *very* important news!

There is a far greater decision than any of these, however, which we must make. Pilate knew it when he said, 'What shall I do with Jesus?' This is life's greatest choice, upon which everything else depends, either for our present and eternal salvation or for our eternal loss. Therefore—What shall the answer be?

The Milk Boy or, *A Habit We Should Form*. He is a

most useful lad, for he brings to us the precious bottles of milk, so necessary for food and body-building. No wonder we frequently see the familiar slogan, 'Drink More Milk,' for it has been proved by health specialists that children who drink pure milk regularly grow up to be taller and healthier than those who don't.

The habit of reading God's Word regularly may be compared likewise with the regular drinking of milk, and the Apostle Peter tells us that this is indeed the secret of growth in the Christian life (1 Peter 2. 2). If we do, then we'll develop into strong, healthy believers, able to walk well in the pilgrim pathway, able to run well in the Christian race, and able to fight well in the fight of faith.

The Schoolboy or, *Lessons We Must Learn.* Here is a boy who has begun to appreciate the value of a good education,

so he has determined to do his very best at school. It means, of course, that he has to sacrifice many an hour when, otherwise, he might be enjoying himself at games, etc. But his eye is on the future, when he hopes to be able to fill an important position in life. It is no surprise, then, to learn later that he has passed his examinations with flying colours, and ultimately reached the goal of his ambition.

In a similar way, when we receive the Saviour, we enter God's School, there to learn important lessons which will enable us to live and work for Him Who died for us. It requires diligent reading of His Word; but, by so doing, we learn own own weakness and His ability; we learn also the great lessons of faith, obedience, service and loyalty, and many other subjects of supreme importance. (Matt. 11. 29).

The Drummer Boy or, *The Battle We Must Fight.* In the old days, before this present century, this lad was a common sight for, at that time, boys were taken into the Army at an early age. Very often they began their career either as a bugler or drummer-boy. When the Army went into action, this lad was frequently in the thick of the fighting, playing a most important part. If he knew how to handle his sticks well, he could give tremendous encouragement to his fellow-soldiers and so help them to win the battle.

It is recorded of a drummer boy in Napoleon's army who turned a defeat into victory. The order was given to 'Beat a Retreat; but this lad stood motionless while his eyes flashed with determination and confidence. Again the command was given, but still he made no move to obey. The officer in charge thundered at him once more, but all to no purpose, Then the lad replied: "Sir, I don't know how, for I was never taught it." "*What* can you beat?" shouted the officer. "Sir," the boy answered with a triumphant ring in his voice, "*I can beat a charge.*" "Then beat it," commanded the officer, and immediately the boy seemed as one inspired, for he beat his drum with such vigour and determination that the soldiers of Napoleon rallied, regained their positions, and finally routed the enemy—thanks largely to this brave drummer boy. And surely that should be the spirit of every young person who has enlisted in the Army of the King of kings.

The drummer boy tells us that it is not a picnic to be a Christian, but it demands courage, self sacrifice and real determination if we are to meet the forces of evil and over-come. In His strength, however, we can win and thus be able to sing—

> *On the victory side,*
> *On the victory side,*
> *With Christ within,*
> *The fight we'll win,*
> *On the victory side.*

Donkeys of the Bible

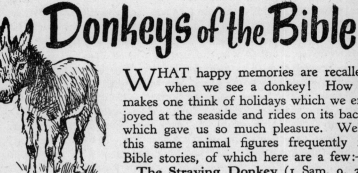

WHAT happy memories are recalled when we see a donkey! How it makes one think of holidays which we enjoyed at the seaside and rides on its back, which gave us so much pleasure. Well, this same animal figures frequently in Bible stories, of which here are a few:—

The Straying Donkey (1 Sam. 9. 3). In this chapter we read the story of several asses which belonged to a man named Kish, whose son, Saul, was sent to find them. Along with a servant this young man travelled from place to place for three days, seeking to find some trace of the lost donkeys, but without success. Then they met the prophet Samuel who told them that the animals had been found; so, with no more anxiety, they returned home to find them all safe and sound.

The chief trait of the donkey is that *it loves its own way.* That is why it likes to roam wherever it chooses. Those who have travelled through the country parts of Ireland will be familiar with the straying donkey, for many are to be seen there, wandering about, and nobody seems to be looking for them! What is true of the straying donkey is likewise true of us all; but the good news of the Gospel declares that Jesus came to seek and to save that which was *lost* (Luke 19. 10).

Nearly every day we read of some child who has mysteriously disappeared and is lost. In many cases we have heard of hundreds and even thousands of people willing to help, combing large areas of the district in order to find the child. Sometimes they succeed, but, alas, not always. The Bible teaches that we have *all* lost our way (Isa. 53. 6), not just some people, therefore we all require a Saviour. But it is a comfort to know that we are just the very people Jesus came to seek and save.

The Sentenced Donkey (Exod. 13. 13). Here is a poor Israelite who possesses a baby donkey but, who has no lamb, and no money to buy one. He knows that the Word of God has declared that every firstling of an ass must die unless a lamb is found to take its place and so redeem it. Let us suppose, however, that a kind friend of his hears of his distress and brings along a lamb which dies instead of the condemned donkey. What rejoicing there is then in this family circle, when they know that their little favourite is now spared!

This story is given so that we might learn that, like the sentenced donkey, we all require a Substitute to take our place, or else we must bear the awful penalty of our sins. How happy we should be then to know that Jesus came as the Lamb of God to become our Substitute and die for us so that we might be spared.

In 'The Tale of Two Cities,' Charles Dickens tells of the sacrifice of Sidney Carton, when he gave his life for his chum. It meant first getting into that horrible Paris prison, then changing clothes and taking his friend's place. Love triumphed over all the difficulties, however, for Sidney Carton died, and thus Charles Darney walked forth a free man. And so may we go free, also, if we accept Christ as our Substitute.

The Speaking Donkey (Num. 22. 28-30). In this story the ass is given the power of speech! It had an unkind master, for though Balaam professed to be a religious man he was really a hypocrite, who wanted to make money for his services. He was asked by the King of Moab to utter a prophetic curse upon God's people, the Israelites, who were then on the march to Canaan. Although God had told Balaam not to go on this visit to the King, he disobeyed; so God sent an angel to reprove him, who appeared in the way with a drawn sword. The prophet did not see the angel at first, however, although the donkey did, and therefore, refused to go forward. At that moment the cruel master hit the ass, and it was then that it was made to say—'What have I done unto thee?' Its master must have been amazed when he was addressed in such a manner by his own donkey! Then Balaam suddenly saw the angel, who declared: 'Unless the ass had turned from me, surely now also I had slain thee and saved her alive.' No wonder the disobedient prophet confessed afterwards, 'I have sinned,' but even then he did not turn back.

Let us note a few things about this donkey—

It had a bad master and suffered much from his cruel treatment, thus making its life one of misery and cruel bondage.

It was prepared to suffer rather than disobey God. It was content to have the blows of its master, rather than go in the wrong direction and face the angel's sword.

It was not afraid to speak the God-given words. Thus it showed remarkable courage to reprove its master and make him think of his folly, and also of the God against whom he was sinning. Surely if a donkey can do these things, how much more should we be prepared to open our mouths for the Lord in glad confession (Rom. 10. 9), and take our stand for the right.

The Serving Donkey (Mark 11. 1-11). There are several occasions in Scripture in which we find this animal rendering splendid service. Abraham and Isaac used it when they went on that memorable journey to Mount Moriah. The good Samaritan, too, in all probability, rode a donkey on the Jericho road, when he discovered and rescued the unfortunate traveller. But perhaps the best story in the New Testament in which the ass figures as a faithful servant is found in Mark 11. 1-11. It is a lesson complete in itself; but, here are a few suggested headings: (1) Jesus wanted it; (2) Jesus sent His servants to find it; (3) It required to be set free; (4) It had to be brought to Jesus; (5) It was perfectly submissive and yielded itself to His control as He rode upon it into the city of Jerusalem. Boys and girls, likewise, are wanted by Jesus for that reason and He has sent forth His servants to bring them to Himself so that they might yield themselves to His control for His service. Then, when He comes as King of kings, He will have them with Him in that wonderful day of majestic glory.

The Cow

IF we think of the rich, creamy milk, butter and cheese which the cow provides for our tables, we should feel very much indebted to it! It is, indeed, a very valuable animal which cannot be done without. Let us, then, observe a few things about it which teach some helpful lessons.

Lost—*It may stray and get lost.* While walking along a country road we may have come across one or two cows which have wandered from the farm. They may be heading for a busy road, where they might be killed. Perhaps a thoughtless boy left a gate open, and the cows fancied that the grass by the roadside was much better than that in the field, so out they went! It was all done so easily and quickly; but, although they know it not, the cows are lost, and require to be sought and brought back to the farm.

One morning, a poor old Chinese Christian woman, who lived alone, missed her cow and knew that it must have been stolen. Immediately she prayed that the Lord would send it back safely, seeing that it was her only means of support. Her prayer was answered in a remarkable way for, at that time, a mist fell on the countryside. An hour or so later, to her great joy, she heard the well-known sound of the cow's bell, and soon afterwards the animal re-appeared. The mist had caused the thieves to lose their way so they had been compelled to let the cow find its own way home lest they should be caught with it. And thus the lost cow came home!

What is true, at times, of the cow is true, likewise, of everyone, for Isa. 53. 6 declares that "All we like sheep have gone astray." We all possess a nature which loves to stray, and that is why we all require a Saviour. Although astray, however we, too, may find the homeward way.

Purchased—*It has an owner* whose name is on the Herd Book. We never find a cow which has no owner, unlike the pit-ponies of Devon, which run wild on the moors. Every cow has an owner and also knows its own master. Isaiah 1. 3 states that 'The ox (or the cow) *knoweth his owner* . . .' Likewise, it is gloriously possible for a boy or girl to be able to say, 'I belong to Jesus'.

A Scottish farmer emigrated to Canada and, after years of hard work, possessed a large farm—but he had forgotten God. One day, while he stood looking over his fields, he placed his hand on a gate-post. Just then, to his surprise, one of his cows came forward and began to lick the back of his hand. Like a flash the words of Isaiah 1. 3 came to mind, 'The ox knoweth his master . . . but Israel doth not know . . .' for he had learned them when he was a boy. It was true that his cow knew him; but he did not know the God who had blessed him so abundantly. The result was that very soon afterwards he sought and found the Saviour and was able to acknowledge Him as his Master.

Sometimes we may happen to see some cows which have just been purchased in the market, with the purchase labels still on their backs. Before these labels were affixed, however, the purchase price had been paid. And before we could be possessed by the Saviour, He had to pay the price of our redemption—and what a price! Purchase involves a change of masters, and this also happens when we come to the Lord Jesus for then He becomes our new Master.

Cleansed—*It must be kept clean.* The Government demands that every cow must be kept in a clean and healthy condition, or else it may spread disease. That is why we hear and read so much about T.T. herds, pasteurised milk, etc., in order that everything connected with the cow may be kept perfectly clean.

Cleansing is also God's first requirement, for He is holy; therefore we must be cleansed from all our sins by the precious blood of Christ if we are ever to enter heaven. Then, there is also the constant, daily cleansing of our minds and ways by the reading of the Scriptures (Eph. 5. 26). Only by so doing are we really happy and able to be of any service for the Master.

A motherless boy had often to wait a long time at night before his father returned home from work. Many an evening was wet, and it was difficult for the child to keep himself clean while playing around outdoors. It was not surprising, then, that one of the first things the father used to say to him was, "Johnny, show me your hands?" and reluctantly they were shown. Then the boy was sent to wash himself before he could sit down with his father at the supper table, or play games with him afterwards. Thus we, too, must be cleansed from our sins before we can enjoy the Father's house and all the blessings of the Glory Land.

Wise—*It possesses good sense.* The cow, as a rule, answers quickly when it is called. I saw this fact proved some time ago when I watched a young farm servant as she went out to call in the cows without even the help of a dog. The cows were out of sight at the time; but, within a few minutes, they came towards her without delay, some of them running, as if glad to be called. The girl knew each one by name and without any effort brought them all in.

Another mark of its good sense is the cow's wise habits when feeding. It is most careful as to what it eats, for it prefers the juicy grass and refuses to eat weeds, etc. It also takes care to lie down while it chews the cud. What a fine example to us! By so doing, it would teach us to feed regularly on the Word of God and thus enjoy our 'quiet time' as we seek to make that Word our own.

There are always exceptions to this rule, however, for some cows seem to eat almost anything, including nails, buttons, wires, etc. As a result they require an operation to have these things removed from their stomach. The lesson, therefore, is *be careful what you eat* and choose that which will make you a strong healthy Christian.

Gentle—*It has a submissive nature.* Unlike the horse, the mule, or the ass, the cow is a quiet animal and is easily led. There is nothing wild about it, or anything which would frighten a child, while, generally, it seems to have no will of its own.

This same submissive spirit should mark every boy and girl who have found the Lord Jesus. It was the spirit of the Master Himself, for He prayed, 'Not my will, but Thine be done'; so we must seek to follow His example, if we would be like Him.

Useful—*It has much to offer.* Just think of the many things with which we are enriched by the cow. These include—milk, cream, butter, cheese, beef from the carcase, leather from the hide; while the horns and hoofs supply such things as knife-handles, buttons, soap, glue, jellies, etc. Thus the cow is always giving supplies for the benefit of others. And surely if we have received so many blessings from the Lord Jesus we should seek to give back something to Him, of our time, talents, or possessions, just like the lad with the loaves and and fishes, so that His name might be honoured and others blessed.

A Treasure Hunt!

WE'RE going to join in a real live Treasure Hunt, and I trust we'll not only discover it, but also claim it and enjoy its riches.

I remember, when only a small boy, looking out of a window in our home late one summer evening. To my amazement, I saw two men digging a hole in a spare piece of ground, where we used to play. I held my breath as I watched them putting a parcel into this hole then cover it up, and finally disappear. It was too late then to go out to investigate, and although several of us searched for it diligently the following days, no trace of the treasure could be found and the mystery was never solved.

Here are three Treasure Stories of the Bible which are most interesting, and from which we may all gather lasting treasure:—

Stolen Treasure (Josh. 7. 20-26). Yonder is a burning city, Jericho, once famed for its beauty, but now in ruins, for God's judgment has fallen upon it. Every inhabitant has perished, except Rahab and her relatives. Although every Israelite has been strictly commanded not to take anything from this condemned city; yet one man dares to defy the Divine order, and steals several things. He buries his treasure and rejoices to think that he has not been seen. His joy is short-lived, however, for Israel is defeated in battle soon afterwards, when they fail to capture the small town of Ai.

It is then that God reveals the cause—'Israel hath sinned . . . and taken of the accursed thing' (v. 11). As a result, God declares solemnly, 'Neither will I be with you any more, except ye destroy the accursed from among you' (v. 12). In the morning the tribes assemble, and the tribe of Judah is selected; then the family of the Zarhites, and finally, the culprit, Achan, is exposed before all.

Listen to his sorrowful confession: '*I saw* among the spoil a goodly Babylonian garment, and 200 shekels of silver, and a wedge of gold of 50 shekels weight. *I coveted* them . . . *I took* . . . *I hid* them in the earth. . . .' This is the man with the Stolen Treasure; who, instead of enriching himself, loses everything, including his own life, for afterwards he is stoned to death for his disobedience and folly.

The lesson of the Stolen Treasure is solemn, yet very necessary. It teaches not only that stealing is a serious sin, but something far more important, namely, that disobedience to God's Word brings its own punishment. May we dare to stand firm, therefore, and say 'No' when we are tempted to disobey and lay hold of Stolen Treasure.

Sought Treasure (Matt. 13. 44). This second story concerns a rich Eastern merchant who spent most of his time seeking for special Treasure which, possibly, had been lost by some rich travellers, who may have been waylaid and robbed. The robbers may have been compelled to bury part of the vast store, intending to return for it later. We can picture this stately sheik as he travelled from place to place seeking to get some information which would put him on the trail. At last he did hear something which gave him a clue, so off he went, and eventually began digging operations. He probably had many difficulties to surmount, many hardships to endure, and many disappointments to overcome; but he never gave up the search until, at long last, while seeking diligently, he saw some shining objects in the ground which proved to be the long-looked-for Treasure. It included all kinds of rare and costly jewels, fit for a royal crown, besides silver and gold in abundance. Before he could claim it, however, he had to sell all his possessions in order to purchase the field in which the Treasure lay. That done the treasure then became his own possession.

In this story the Seeker is a picture of the Saviour, who came from the heights of Glory to this sinful world, that He might seek and find the richest possible Treasure. It was not silver and gold which He sought, but *living* Treasure, boys and girls of every land, and grown-ups too. For these—for us—He gave His all, even life itself, that He might find and possess the gems that will adorn His glorious crown in that day when He makes up His jewels.

In the middle of last century, an old settler was digging a trench near the Sacramento River, not dreaming that the next stroke of his spade was to influence the history of the world. His wondering eyes soon discovered certain shining particles among the sand which he soon recognised as gold. The bewildering news thrilled the heart of North America and far beyond it. Thirty thousand Americans crossed the plains, climbed the mountains, bore without shirking all the want, exposure, fatigue, danger from attack by Indians, and plodded over more than 2,000 miles of unexplored wilderness towards their goal—and gold. *But* 4,000 *died on the way*; 50,000 came by sea from different countries, and before the year was out, 80,000 had come to hunt for golden treasure in California.

Such is the sacrifice that men will make if they think they can find earthly treasure; but, even though it be secured, it cannot buy real joy, or purchase eternal salvation. How glad we should be, then, to know that Christ paid all the price so that we might become His eternal Treasure!

Shared Treasure (2 Kings 7. 8-11). It is a time of war and famine in Israel. The enemy has invaded and plundered the land, leaving the people in a desperate, famishing condition. Lying outside the gate of the city of Samaria are four lepers, faced with a terrible death. So awful is their plight that they determine to appeal to the invading Syrians for bread; but, to their amazement, they discover that the enemy has suddenly fled, leaving behind them many valuable stores of food, silver, gold, and raiment. With difficulty, these plague-stricken men go from tent to tent, scarcely believing what they see! Their first thought is for themselves, so they enjoy a good meal before starting to bury some of the supplies. They wait for some time, but still the enemy does not return; so they talk together as to what they should do with the Treasure. To sit there and enjoy themselves while their friends starve to death is more than they dare to contemplate, so they decide to *share the Treasure*. Noble men! Then, with four fine horses they ride off to tell the good news, with the result that the starving people partake of the supplies and are saved as if by a miracle.

David Livingstone was one who acted in a similar manner. While only a lad in his 'teens, he came to know of God's great Treasure in the Gospel; but, no sooner did he discover it than he decided to share it. He had heard a little of the vast needs of Africa, then known as the 'Dark Continent,' and determined if possible, to take the Gospel Treasure to its peoples. The visitor to the Scottish National Memorial to David Livingstone at his birthplace, Blantyre, may read, among his letters there, the one he wrote to the Missionary Society offering himself as a prospective missionary to Africa. Thus he went forth, shortly afterwards, to open up that vast continent and share the Treasure with those who had never heard of God's wondrous love.

Another intrepid missionary who followed in Livingstone's train was Frederick Stanley Arnot. When he was only a boy of six years of age he heard Livingstone giving an account of his travels and vowed that he, too, would go to Africa—even if he had to swim to get there! Possessed with the same spirit of courage and self-sacrifice as his leader, he gave himself, likewise, for Africa and thus shared the heavenly Treasure. And surely we, too, should seek to share it.

Faces False and Real

MOST children enjoy playing with false faces, especially at Hallowe'en. What fun they provide, and how difficult it is to know just who is who! Well, here are a number of different faces which tell at a glance something of the character of the person represented:—

A Black Face (Jer. 13. 23). Everyone can guess that this boy is a *real* negro, and not just someone wearing a false face!

He was born of negro parents, and therefore possesses the same nature and the same dark skin as they. It is not because he has been playing with mud that his skin is black, but rather because he was born a negro. Suppose, however, that Sambo decides to try and whiten his skin. He buys soap and brushes, then, with a plentiful supply of hot water, he begins 'the big scrub.' At first he thinks he is succeeding, so he rubs harder. But it is all a failure for, after all his efforts, he is no different. The Ethiopian *cannot* change his skin; neither can anyone cleanse away their sin-stains by reformation, good works, or any other personal effort, though they may be ever so sincere.

A coloured man in Central America heard of a certain remedy which, it was claimed, made black skins white. He bought it and read the instructions. One powder a day was supposed to be taken; but this was far too slow a process for him, so he quickly swallowed all the powders at once! As a result he nearly lost his life; but when he recovered some weeks later, he discovered, to his great joy, that his skin had changed colour and was nearly white. He still had his negro features, however, for these could not be changed. How like many people who try to appear as though they had cleansed themselves of their sins, yet, underneath, there is still the same old sinful nature!

A Disguised Face (2 Kings 9. 30). This chapter tells of how Jehu, King of Israel, came to seek out Jezebel, the wicked

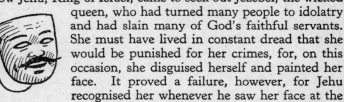

queen, who had turned many people to idolatry and had slain many of God's faithful servants. She must have lived in constant dread that she would be punished for her crimes, for, on this occasion, she disguised herself and painted her face. It proved a failure, however, for Jehu recognised her whenever he saw her face at the window, and quickly brought her to judgment. It is a solemn story of the deceitfulness of the human heart, and also, of the justice of God, from which the sinner cannot escape; though he may use many disguises.

Jacob was another who believed in the use of disguise, and employed it to deceive his old dying father so that he would obtain the blessing; which, by rights, belonged to his older brother Esau. He brought a savoury dish and pretended to his father that it was venison, while, in reality, it was only goat's flesh. He disguised his hands and neck also by putting on skins, for he knew that his brother was a hairy man and expected that his father would feel his neck and hands, which he did. Thus, by deceit and disguise, he stole the father's blessing; but it cost him twenty years' separation from home in the far country; while he never saw his parents again.

Thus we learn that *disguises do not pay*, for no one can cheat God.

A Sulky Face (Luke 15. 28-30). How often this unpleasant face makes its appearance! It is not only children who 'go into the sulks', for we read here of a young man who was guilty of this same fault. He was the older brother of the Prodigal Son, who had just been forgiven by his father and welcomed back to the old home. The joy was overflowing; the feast was spread; everyone was celebrating the happy occasion—except this sulking brother. Seeing the empty chair, the father went out to the field and pled with the older son to join with them, but the young man stubbornly refused. He was too proud to sit beside his pardoned brother: and, in reality, was a far greater prodigal himself, for he spurned his father's love and would not repent. Let us beware, then, of this sulking face!

A Hidden Face (Luke 19. 4). Perhaps we have seen a boy who has been caught while doing something naughty. In all

probability, he covers his face, lest anyone should recognise him and tell his parents. 'Conscience doth make cowards of us all,' wrote Shakespeare, and where there is a sense of guilt there is usually a sense of fear also. It is only to be expected, then, that the guilty one should try to hide his face.

Zacchaeus was another who sought to hide his face, although, in his case, it was because of his timidity rather than from a sense of guilt. He belonged to the hated class of tax-gatherers and did not want to be seen with Jesus, lest he should be recognised and, in all likelihood, criticised by the people. But he was *very* anxious to see Jesus, nevertheless, so he dared to climb a sycamore tree, just like a boy, in order to hide himself among the leaves. Then, while he looked down he realised that he was seen, for the penetrating eyes of the Saviour were fastened upon him. He felt that he was known, too, for Jesus called him by name. It seems that all his fears vanished at that moment, for he descended from his hiding place at once and gladly received the Lord Jesus. Of course he was criticised; but he did not mind that, for he had found the secret of real joy. It was no wonder, then, that he invited Jesus to his home and many of his friends also, so that they might be introduced to the Saviour. Such was the little man who, only a short time before, had been hiding from Jesus!

A Happy Face (Psa. 32. 1). If sin brings sadness, salvation brings gladness, and it cannot be hidden for the face soon betrays the secret of the joy within. David, in this passage, exclaims: 'O the happiness of the man whose transgression is forgiven, whose sin is covered!' This is true, likewise, in the experience of everyone who receives Divine forgiveness.

A young girl sat in a Sunday School in Toronto, listening to a message which gripped her heart and enabled her to trust the Saviour there and then. She thought, however, that she would keep it a secret; but, after a few days, she ran to her mother, threw her arms around her neck and, with beaming face, exclaimed: "Oh, Mummie, I've got a secret which I can't keep any longer." Then she related what had happened. The mother was not altogether surprised, however, for the secret had already been revealed—in her face!

A Shining Face (Acts 6. 15). In chapters six and seven of the book of the Acts, we read of Stephen, the first Christian martyr, who was brought before the same Jewish leaders who had condemned the Lord Jesus. They acted in exactly the same manner towards him, falsely accusing and condemning him; but fearlessly he stood up for his Lord and charged his accusers with being guilty of putting Jesus to death (7. 52). As he faced these bitter enemies 'his face shone as that of an angel,' for it was radiant with a heavenly glory.

A Hindu trader in Kherwana market once asked a Christian convert: "What medicine do you put on your face to make it shine so? I've seen it in Agra, Surat, and Bombay." Penna laughed as he said: "Yes, I'll tell you the medicine; *it is happiness of heart*." Likewise, if we seek to stand true and faithful for our Lord as Stephen and Penna did, and many others, then our faces will, in some measure, shine with His glory. And nothing is so attractive and so convincing as the shining face!

Five Bible Girls

WE are going to form an acrostic, using the word GIRLS, linking each letter with a girl mentioned in the Scriptures. The first is the letter 'G', so we'll turn to Matt. 26. 69, where we read of:—

A Girl Who Was Guilty. She was the maid who noticed Peter, after he came inside the palace of the High Priest, just after Christ had been arrested. She knew from his appearance and accent that he was from Galilee; so she supposed that he must have been a follower of Jesus. 'Thou also wast with Jesus of Galilee,' she said, while Peter felt most uncomfortable by these challenging words as he stood warming himself at the fire beside the enemies of his Master. Though she was only a maid who had so addressed him Peter had no courage to say, 'Yes, that is true, and I'm not ashamed to own Him as my Lord.' Instead he played the coward, then covered his cowardice with lies. As for the girl, she was guilty of taking her stand against the Saviour, guilty also of influencing others around her to do likewise. Worst of all, she was guilty of causing this favoured disciples to fall into grievous sin. If she lived today in all probability she would say to the believer, 'Oh, you are one of these despised Christians, aren't you?' Then she would probably laugh and mock.

During the Second World War, a young soldier received a letter from his former Bible Class leader, pleading with him to yield himself to Christ. In reply, he wrote these solemn words: "I have made my decision; but *it is not the decision you wanted me to make*, for I don't think it is possible to be a Christian in the Army." He was just like this guilty girl.

The second letter 'I' tells of:—

A Girl Who Was Interested (2 Kings 5). Of all girls mentioned in the Bible, this one is probably the best known, though her name is not given. In the first place, *she was interested in God's Word*. She knew a good deal about the true God and His faithful servants who had lived down through the centuries. No doubt her mother was her teacher, and we can picture her sitting on her mother's knee, listening intently to the great Bibles stories. *She was interested in her own spiritual condition* also, for, although only a child, she believed in her mother's God and trusted Him as her God, too. *She was interested in others* also, for when she heard of Naaman's hopeless condition she immediately told her mistress where a sure cure could be found.

A young Ayrshire lad of about ten years of age wrote the following words in a letter to the gentleman who had addressed a children's meeting which he had attended: 'I really have been doing my best to follow the Lord Jesus Christ, and *I do wish my companions would come to Him as well.*' At the close of that meeting he had come forward and said boldly: 'I want to believe on the Saviour,' and his letter proved that, not only had he done so, but also showed his interest in the salvation of his chums.

The third letter, 'R' tells of—

A Girl Who Was Raised (Mark 5. 21-43). When Peter's boat was returning from across the Lake of Galilee, a welcoming crowd met Jesus and His disciples as they stepped ashore. Among them was a well-known and important person named Jairus, one of the chief rulers in the local synagogue. With a look of distress he appealed to the Master to come at once and heal his daughter, for she was sinking fast. The Lord agreed to return with him to his home; but the vast crowd thronged Him and delayed Him so much that, when He arrived at this home, the little girl was dead. The house was filled with mourners who made doleful noises, so He put them all outside; then took the parents and His three favoured disciples, Peter, James and John with Him into the room where the girl lay. Then, without any delay He addressed the little one thus: 'Little maid, I say to you, Arise!' Her big, wondering eyes opened at once, as she looked into the face of the Saviour, while the others stood amazed. Then the Lord Jesus delivered her into the care of her mother and requested that she should be given something to eat. No wonder, therefore, that we read, 'They were astonished with a great astonishment.'

Likewise, Jesus is still saying to boys and girls, 'Arise!' and giving life everlasting to all who hear His Word and believe on Him.

That brings us to the letter 'L' and to—

A Girl Who Was Listening (Acts 12. 13, 14). Her name was Rhoda, which means 'Rose'. She was probably employed in this home of the mother of John Mark. At that time the Apostle Peter was lying in prison, while Herod the king had planned his execution for the following day. That was why the Christians had gathered together here to have an all-night prayer meeting on Peter's behalf. They asked God to spare the life of His valued servant and leader of His people. While they prayed God heard and answered for an angel was sent at once on a special mission to deliver Peter from prison, and from all his enemies. In a most wonderful way he accomplished this, and finally parted from Peter just outside the prison gates. It was then that the apostle thought of this home where, on earlier occasions, he must have been a frequent visitor. But never before had he ever called there at such an early hour. At that moment Rhoda heard his knock, and perhaps recognised it as Peter's usual knock. Then, while the others were still praying, she ran to the door and recognised Peter standing before her. Instead of bringing him inside at once, however, she ran back and informed the others, who refused to believe her, for it was more than they had ever expected. But soon they were compelled to believe that Peter had been delivered, for they saw him for themselves and heard from his own lips the story of his wonderful deliverance. Then they rejoiced together and gave thanks to God for answered prayer.

Rhoda still lives! She is as fragrant as a rose and is ever on the alert, ever ready to hear the knock, ready to carry the good news, ready to serve in the home, ready to join with others in prayer, ready to do anything she can to help others. No wonder, then, that she is specially mentioned in the Scriptures!

Finally, the letter 'S' tells us of:—

A Girl Who Was Steadfast (Exod. 2. 3, 4). Her name was Miriam, the sister of Moses, who kept watch over him when he lay as a helpless babe in the ark by the River Nile. The King of Egypt had decreed that every baby boy born to the Israelites was to die; but the parents of Moses refused to obey this order. It was then that the wonderful idea of putting the baby inside the special basket was all thought out and at last, late one evening, or very early one morning, they carried the little one down to the river's edge and left him there. Miriam remained to stand guard over him and to see what happened until, finally, the baby boy was discovered in the morning by the princess and eventually delivered. Let us observe, then, that Miriam was an *obedient* girl. She was also an *unselfish* girl. She was a *brave* girl, too, for she ran a grave risk, and might have had to suffer severely if the secret had been revealed. She was a *wise* girl, likewise, for she kept out of sight until the baby was discovered. Above all, she was a *loving* girl, for she loved the Lord, loved her parents, loved her baby brother, and loved her people. If Miriam had failed to do her duty that night, we might never have heard of Moses and all his mighty work, and what a tremendous loss that would have been! But because she was steadfast, she was *rewarded* and had the joy of seeing her brother become her people's deliverer. What a fine example Miriam presents to us of out-and-out loyalty of heart to the Lord!

Boots and Shoes

IT has been said that 'shoes have tongues, but cannot speak,' but that is not altogether true for they can teach us some practical lessons:—

A New Shoe and its Perfection. This shoe has just been purchased and is therefore without any signs of wear, or even a speck of dust to spoil its appearance. It is just as it came from its maker, well designed, well-built, and made with the very best of materials.

With all its perfection it would suggest to us the first man, Adam, as he came from the Hand of God, faultless and perfect. It would also remind us of his wonderful joy as he *walked* with God in the beautiful Garden of Eden, before sin entered the world, when everything was perfect in that Paradise of bliss.

A Tramp's Boot and its Ruin. What a contrast it presents to the first shoe! This one has been worn until it has practically fallen to pieces and is of no further use. The sole has a gaping hole in it, the upper is burst, while the heel has almost disappeared!

If the first shoe speaks of man in his innocence, this one surely portrays him in his fallen state as a sinner, ruined and perishing. There is no use trying to patch him up with good works and the like. What he requires is a new life altogether.

George Goodman used to tell an imaginary tale of a poor tramp, who lay outside Buckingham Palace watching the distinguished visitors come and go. Then one day he picked up a card which one of the special visitors had dropped accidentally. It was an invitation to a royal banquet; so, from that moment he was seen busily engaged sewing and patching his ragged garments in order that he might be able to join the favoured company! What folly! and yet that is just what many people are doing today, trying to fit themselves for the presence of the King of kings by patching up their lives, etc., instead of being born again.

A Wellington Boot and its Protection. This boot is made, not to be worn on sunny days but on stormy ones, when rain, sleet, or snow may come. That is the time when we require to be properly protected, and particularly our feet, for wet feet may quickly cause chills and serious illness. Inside this coloured wellington there is a warm lining also, thus providing comfort as well as protection. It will be noticed, too, that this is a child's wellington, for little ones, also, require to be protected from the perils of storm and winter.

The lesson of the wellington is that protection is guaranteed in the Gospel. There are storms of temptation and testing now, which we may have to encounter; while there is also the coming storm of Divine judgment which every unsaved one must face unless they have found protection and salvation in Christ. Noah learned this same lesson and found protection inside the Ark; so, likewise, all who flee to Christ for salvation are sheltered and placed beyond the reach of judgment (John 5. 24).

A Skating Boot and its Test. This is a boot which many young people love to possess—unless those who live in the tropics, or in countries where there is no ice! Often we may hear a boy remark, 'I wish it were skating time again!' There are a number of young folks, however, who seem to think that they could never learn to skate, simply because they lack confidence and yet they envy all those who can skate! It may appear difficult to learn; but, in reality, it is not, provided the skater has a good pair of boots and skates.

There must be a willingness on the part of the skater, however, to put on the skates, to trust the ice to bear his or her whole weight, and then to venture forth.

This is a splendid illustration of faith, for, just as the skater must trust both the ice and the skates so the Christian starts his or her Christian life by trusting Christ. As the confidence of the skater increases by constant exercise, so similarly the faith of the believer grows stronger by constant use. The skater, too, has great joy (even though there may be an occasional fall!) so, likewise, the Christian rejoices as faith in Christ is repeatedly exercised.

The Military Boot and its Strength. This boot is made for hard wear and long life, for it belongs to a soldier on active

service. It bears the Government stamp and also a number, so that anyone who sees it may know that it is a military boot issued to a soldier after his enlistment in the Army of the Queen. It has stood up to the test of many long route-marches over rough country; though its wearer did feel his feet tired and sore at times; but not as sore as they would have been if he had not possessed such good footwear.

This military boot would suggest to us that if we have chosen Christ as Saviour, we are *soldiers* of the King of kings, volunteers and not merely conscripts; because we want to do His will and serve under His banner. This new life demands constant *obedience*, for the boot can only tread in the appointed path, and not just where the soldier wants to go. It means *endurance*, too, and *loyalty* as we seek to follow wherever our Commander leads. (John 21. 22).

The Climber's Boot and its Grip. One glance at this particular boot tells us that it belongs to a mountaineer.

It has been made specially for the purpose of scaling steep, slippery tracks and precipitous heights. Such a task requires proper footwear which will grip the ground firmly and thus prevent slipping and

possible disaster. If this spiked boot could speak, it might tell some thrilling tales of daring adventures in Switzerland, or other mountainous country where several great heights were climbed, and many dangers and difficulties conquered—thanks largely to the boots.

The Christian, likewise, should be a good climber. There are many steep places to climb, just as Pilgrim had to ascend the Hill Difficulty. There are great mountains to be scaled also, but this feat cannot be accomplished unless the climber is properly shod. Otherwise there might be slipping and, possibly, a disastrous fall. If we read God's Word diligently, however, it will enable us to climb safely for it will give us a good, firm grip of the track on our upward way and thus prevent slipping. We must also follow our Guide closely, and never attempt to go without Him, as so many climbers are tempted to do at times, and very often come to grief. Thus we'll be able to sing as we go—

> *Climb, climb up sunshine mountain,*
> *Heavenly breezes blow.*

The Wedding Shoe and its Beauty. In contrast to the other footwear, this lovely shoe is made specially for one particular day, for it is a bride's shoe which she will wear on that eventful and happy wedding day.

Just as the bride looks forward with eager anticipation to that wonderful day of supreme happiness and seeks to prepare herself in every way for it, so the believer, likewise, should anticipate with joy and preparation of life the Marriage Supper of the Lamb in heavenly glory (Rev. 19. 7). Then our union with Himself will be celebrated by all the redeemed in that wondrous scene of unsullied purity and beauty. This shoe would tell us that, because Jesus suffered and died to put away our sins, we shall *stand* in His presence then, 'faultless and stainless, safe in that happy land.'

(Another shoe may be added from Lesson No. 16).

Familiar Sayings

THERE are a number of well-known sayings that we use frequently which give a word-picture of what we desire to say. For instance, we may employ this expression:—

As Red as a Beetroot. Let us suppose that a schoolmaster, just before an examination, gives a warning to his

class that they must not copy. There is one lad, however, who has not been doing his work well, and who cannot possibly hope to succeed on his own merits; so he dares to disobey the order. At the end of the examination the master happens to see this lad who, by his very appearance, betrays his guilt. He is then questioned as to whether he obeyed the order, then suddenly his face turns a vivid colour and becomes '*as red as a beetroot!*'

This expression suggests the thought of the guilty person being found out, such as we have in the case of King David, when Nathan the prophet exposed to him his sin and said, 'Thou art the man' (2 Sam. 12. 7). Achan, Haman, and many others also might be mentioned as those who likewise were found out. How much better it is when, instead of being

found out we confess our sin to God and seek His forgiveness (1 John 1. 9). Then we need have no more fear of being discovered and of having a face '*as red as a beetroot.*'

As Black as Coal. Only those who have been down a coal-mine, or have seen miners as they came from work have any idea what it means to be '*as black as coal.*' The coal dust penetrates so thoroughly through all their clothes and fills all the pores of their bodies that they appear like negroes!

Sometimes we may hear a mother use this expression when speaking to her little boy who, maybe, has been playing in the garden, or in a muddy park or, perhaps, has fallen on a dirty road. His lovely new suit may be covered with mud, while his hands and face are very dirty.

As coal dust makes the miner black, and as mud makes the child black, so, likewise, sin defiles and makes the sinner black. How glad we should be, therefore, to avail ourselves of the means of cleansing in the blood of Christ (1 John 1. 7).

As White as a Sheet. Dr. F. B. Meyer was visiting a lady in Leicester one wintry afternoon, when he noticed a line of

newly washed clothes hanging out to dry. After making a complimentary remark as to their whiteness, he observed the sky becoming overcast. Suddenly snow began to fall and quickly covered the ground. As the lady looked at her clothes, they appeared a dirty, greyish colour, in contrast to the beautiful white snow. Then she exclaimed: "Who can stand against the Almighty's whiteness!"

'*As white as a sheet*' may not be so very white, for all our attempts to appear white and sinless before God may be no better than this woman's efforts at perfect purity. Our *best* endeavours are compared with filthy rags in God's sight (Isa. 64. 6); so, instead of being '*as white as a sheet*' we should seek perfect cleansing and be made 'whiter than the snow' (Psalm 51. 7).

As Slow as a Snail. We have never heard of a snails' race;

but it might be an interesting experiment to try it out—if one had plenty of time! We would require lots of patience, too, for after all each one would only be able to move '*as slow as a snail.*'

Possibly we have met people to whom this expression may truly be applied, who are slow to get up in the morning, slow to learn their lessons, or do their work during the day, and slow to go to bed at night. They have but one speed all the time—dead slow!

There are many young people, likewise, who, when they

hear the Saviour calling them to trust and follow Him, instead of responding at once, keep delaying the matter and saying, 'There's plenty of time.' As far as making up their minds and coming to a definite decision for Christ is concerned, they are *as slow as a snail.*

As Bold as a Lion. While Addressing a Sunday School in Glasgow some time ago, I was amazed to see a girl rise from

her seat near the back of the hall and walk down the aisle towards me. When I enquired as to the reason of her action, she replied, "I want to trust the Saviour *now.*" She could not wait until the address was finished,

so, after a few minutes' talk, she gladly accepted the Lord Jesus as her Saviour. The remarkable feature in her case was that she had been the worst behaved girl in the school; but from that afternoon she became 'as bold as a lion' for her Lord. I met her a few years afterwards and she was still going on brightly for her Lord.

This expression suggests the quality of courage. Just as the lion knows no fear, and can boldly face all the other wild beasts of the forest; so, likewise, all who believe on the Lord Jesus should take their stand for Him, bravely and boldly, though there may be many enemies around them.

As Safe as the Bank. Perhaps you know the chorus, 'Safe am I.' It is grand to be able to sing it with the *heart*, for the

Christian knows that he or she, is not only 'as safe as the Bank,' but very much safer. The main idea in this expression is that of security and protection from all evil powers. This is beautifully illustrated by the Lord in His parable of the Lost Sheep (Luke 15. 3-7). If that rescued sheep could have spoken it might have used the same words as those of the chorus above, for the shepherd not only saved it from perishing, but he also placed it on his strong shoulders and carried it all the way home. Similarly, this is what the Good Shepherd does for every boy or girl who trusts Him. As someone has expressed it, 'He is an all-the-way-home Saviour,' for He saves, keeps, cares, carries, feeds and protects each of His sheep all the journey home. In John 10. 28 we hear Him say: 'I give unto My sheep eternal life, and *they shall never perish.*'

When I lived in Toronto I visited a Safety Deposit Vault along with a friend. There was a large circular steel door of immense thickness, with its many intricate locks, which was opened to us. Inside there were rows of small drawers, where valuables were deposited and these were protected by more locks. This strong-room existed for one purpose only, namely, to provide the best possible protection and security so that anyone might deposit their valuables there with perfect confidence and know they would be kept *'as safe as the Bank.'*

Surely if men can offer such protection and security to those who trust them; then, it is only to be expected that the Lord will offer perfect protection and security to all who trust Him

As Brown as a Berry. Here are Dorothy and Tom, who have just returned from their summer holidays at the seaside

 and both look *'as brown as a berry.'* The reason is that they have lived in the sunshine most of the time and thus have become sun-tanned. How healthy they look and how happy! This expression, then, is associated with the thought of sunshine and joy.

This is something which should be true, likewise, of every Christian as we seek to live in the sunshine of God's love and in the joy of His presence. Then the sunshine will be reflected in our faces and in our lives as we carry it with us everywhere we go.

Four Interesting Ships

E VERY child loves to visit the ships in the harbour of a busy seaport, and, if possible, to be taken on board and shown around. Well, here are a few ships to inspect:—

The Dredger—*To Clear the Way.* When the giant ships, *Queen Mary* and *Queen Elizabeth* were nearly ready for

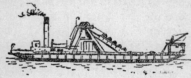

launching, there were a number of these valuable little ships working away at full pressure. The river Clyde is very narrow, and it had to be dredged so that there would be sufficient depth of water for the 'Queens' otherwise they would have stuck in the mud. How like God's salvation. Before we could start off on the voyage of life for the Glory Land, the way had to be cleared. Sin is very much like mud. It is hateful and defiling; it is also a barrier which separates the sinner from God. But the message of the Gospel is that 'He put away sin by the sacrifice of Himself' (Heb. 9. 26). Now the way is clear and we may start off for Heaven and Home.

The Pilot Ship—*To Show the Way.* Suppose we are sailing from a very large city to a distant land. We are shown all

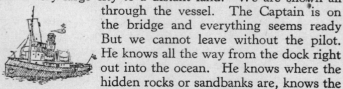

through the vessel. The Captain is on the bridge and everything seems ready But we cannot leave without the pilot. He knows all the way from the dock right out into the ocean. He knows where the hidden rocks or sandbanks are, knows the depth of the water, and every little detail far better than the

Captain. Here he is now! We can see him going right up to the bridge and taking control. Within a short time we are off. The Captain is by his side and the Pilot is showing him the exact way. Presently the little Pilot ship comes alongside and we 'drop the Pilot.' His services are no longer required because he has shown us the way.

We sometimes sing, 'Do you want a Pilot?' Well, we cannot do better than 'bid Him come on board.' The Pilot is the Lord Himself, for He alone knows all the dangers and is competent to take control. Our Pilot, unlike the usual pilot, never requires to leave the ship, but stays on the bridge all the time guiding us safely home.

The Liner—*To Sail Away.* This great ship was not built just to be admired like a pretty picture. It was built at great

cost so that it might sail away carrying its valuable cargo and passengers to another land. The Gospel Ship, too, has been built at great cost—the blood of Christ —so that we might be taken safely over the ocean of life to the Better Land. Look at its *Size*. It is so big that it can take all who come. It is the 'Whosoever' ship (John 3. 16). Look at its *Strength*. It is unsinkable. All the winds and the waves of difficulties and dangers make no difference to it, for it sails on majestically. Look at its *Supplies*. There is abundance, but it cannot be enjoyed unless we step aboard. We must trust ourselves to the One who died for us, before we can enjoy the blessings of His salvation. But, before we go aboard, we must have a ticket. We read of Jonah, the runaway prophet, when he was about to embark for Tarshish that "he paid the fare". The traveller on the Gospel ship, however, learns that if he is prepared to trust the Captain he may have a free ticket because He Himself has paid for it when He died for our salvation. It is a wonderful gift and all He asks is that we accept it and thank Him.

Another unique thing about the Gospel ship is that it is the only one which guarantees a safe passage. We read in

Psalm 107. 30 that "He bringeth them unto their desired haven." Surely that should inspire our confidence and make us want to journey on this wonderful ship. What a wonderful experience! and what a glorious destination!

The Tug—*To Pull Away*. This powerful little ship can do a grand bit of work and teach us a few lessons. Yonder is

a big liner lying in the river. It can't move under its own power, so it calls for assistance. Presently there are several of these little helpers puffing and blowing, pulling the giant ship along into the deep channel until she can sail unaided.

If we have trusted Christ, we ought to be like the tug, *always ready to lend a hand*. We should be ready for service (Rom. I. 15), ready to do His will, no matter how small or how difficult the task. Many a ship would be wrecked if the tugs were not at hand to pull it away off the rocks or sandbanks. So may we, likewise, render a similar service to that of the tug. We may give others a strong 'pull' to Jesus, off the sandbanks of doubt and fear, into the safe channel of peace. Others again may have stuck on the sandbanks of difficulty, or temptation, who, with a helpful tug at hand, would be delivered. Thus may we 'pull away' in the good work of serving the Lord and helping others to Him.

Reference can also be made to the Light-ship—*To Illumine the Way* as it presents a fine illustration of the boy or girl who shines for Jesus and who, by his or her bright testimony, leads others past the dangers into the harbour of eternal safety.

> *Shining all the time, shining all the time,*
> *Shining for Jesus, beams of love divine;*
> *Glorifying Him every day and hour,*
> *Shining all the time for Jesus.*

A RUNAWAY!

(Jonah 1. 1-17; 3. 1-4, 10).

OUR story concerns a *real* person and not merely an imaginary character, for the Lord Himself spoke of Jonah as such. His story is true to life in every detail, and that is what makes it so very interesting. In order, therefore, to link together our headings, we have chosen the little word, **UP**, so, in the first place we observe:—

He was Called Up, not for military service, but, better still, for the service of God. There was special work which He wanted Jonah to do; but, before he could perform it, he had to listen to God's voice and answer His call.

It was a Divine Call, for it was God Himself Who called him. This is what made the matter so very important. If a king calls one of his subjects he dare not refuse, for a royal invitation is virtually a command. How much more so, then, is a Divine order.

It was an Urgent Call, for he was wanted at once, seeing that thousands of people in Nineveh were in danger of perishing, without anyone to warn them of their peril, or tell them of the true God.

It was a Personal Call, for it was specially addressed to Jonah, just as the call of Samuel, Moses, Zacchaeus, Saul of Tarsus and many others was personal. In a similar way the Saviour calls us individually to Himself and says: 'Him that cometh unto Me I will in no wise cast out' (John 6. 37).

Next, we note that—**He Packed Up**. Picture this unhappy man as he gathered together a few articles of clothing

and food to take with him on this strange journey. He wanted
to travel lightly so that he could move freely without any
hindrance. Perhaps this small bundle of personal belongings
spoke to his conscience as he tied it together, and said, "You
are foolish in trying to run away from God, for *it can't be
done.*" Like the Prodigal Son, however, he thought he knew
better, so determined to have his own way. Thus, the lug-
gage of Jonah suggests the separation which follows sin, for
he soon became a homeless wanderer.

Then we see how—**He Hurried Up.** In verse 3 we read,
'But Jonah rose up *to flee* unto Tarshish. . . .' It was not the

usual speed of the Eastern traveller,
but more like the rush of the American!
He resembles one who was flying for
his life, like a person fleeing from a
prairie fire or from a wild animal.
Strange sight, indeed, he must have
presented as he ran from the God who wanted to bless him!

When at last he reached Joppa—**He Paid Up.** Jonah
must have imagined that everything was in his favour, for the
boat was there, as if by special appointment, so that all he had
to do was pay the fare and get on board. This was quickly
paid, for he did not seem to have any shortage of money.
(It might have been better for him if he had not had so much!)
Someone has said: 'There are no free tickets on board the
devil's ship,' a saying which Jonah found to be true indeed.
The money was the smallest part of the cost which he was
compelled to pay, however, for he lost everything he had
brought with him and nearly lost his life besides.

Sin is always an expensive thing, for all who refuse to hear
the Divine Call and prefer to go their own way must be pre-

pared to pay the price, both in
this life and in the life to come.

Afterwards we see how—
He Was Wakened Up. The
runaway was so exhausted that
when he reached the bottom of
the ship, in his efforts to hide

himself, he lay down and fell fast asleep. When the fearful storm arose soon afterwards, and the ship was nearly broken to pieces by its fury, the captain and crew, after much searching, discovered Jonah—still sleeping. Then they proceeded to arouse him to consciousness and told him that he was the cause of all the trouble.

Just as Jonah required to be awakened from his slumber, so the sinner also must be aroused to see his or her great danger if they are ever to be saved from perishing, even though the awakening process may not be very pleasant!

A twelve-year-old boy named John Guthrie, who loved ships, went down to play at the harbour of his native town on the East Coast of Scotland. He climbed aboard a fishing yawl, fell asleep on a pile of nets, and finally was wakened up by the skipper when the ship was 70 miles out to sea. The lad rubbed his eyes and could not believe that he had been at sea for seven hours, during which time his father and police had been searching everywhere for him. Fortunately the skipper was able to flash a message to Arbroath by means of the ship's short-wave set telling that John was safe and well though the sea was rough. That sleep might have cost him his life, for the nets were being shot and he might easily have slipped into the sea and lost his life. Like Jonah, however, his awakening proved to be a great blessing.

Further, we see how—**He Owned Up**. While the angry waves were dashing in all their fury against the ship, and everything looked as if the vessel would founder, the runaway made a full confession of his sin. He took the blame of all the trouble, and was willing to bear the punishment too. It demanded great courage to do so; but he made no excuses for himself whatsoever, unlike so many others when they are found out. 1 John 1. 9 says, 'If we *confess* our sins, He is faithful and just to forgive us our sins,' and that is exactly what Jonah did.

Then—**He Was Lifted Up**. Jonah had just said to the sailors, 'Take me up, and cast me forth into the sea,' so, while the wind howled, and the waves dashed over the ship, 'they took up Jonah and cast him into the sea.' Immediately the

waves ceased their raging and all was calm. But the miracle did not end there, for at that very moment, Jonah was swallowed by a great fish and preserved alive in this strange dwelling for three days and three nights.

It was then that—**He Was Brought Up.** At one word from its Creator and Lord, the fish obeyed by swimming near to the shore, and vomiting up Jonah on to the land. What a terrifying experience it must have been for him to be shut up in the stomach of the fish, and tossed about as it swam through the waters! No wonder, then, that he prayed for deliverance! Although Jonah was under the waves when he cried, yet God heard him and saved him with a wonderful deliverance. Likewise, the Lord will hear and deliver all those who call upon Him and will save them with a more wonderful salvation than that of Jonah.

Lastly—**He Stood Up.** He was given the opportunity once more to go to Nineveh, and this time he chose to go and deliver God's message of warning, 'Forty days and Nineveh shall be overthrown.' The results were startling, for everyone listened to his preaching from the king down to the poorest of his subjects, and immediately believed his message. Then they humbled themselves before God, and cried for mercy. Thus the city which had been marked for judgment was spared through the preaching of Jonah, because he dared to stand up for his Lord.

An American minister, Dudley A. Tyng, a beloved leader in the Y.M.C.A. work in Philadelphia, lay dying after an accident. His last message to the young men was this: 'Tell them to stand up for Jesus. ' George Duffield was thereby led to write the stirring hymn, '*Stand up, stand up for Jesus.*' So let us be UP and doing, gladly yielding ourselves to Him for His royal service.

A Red Cross Lesson

(John 5. 1-16).

MANY Sunday Schools observe one Sunday in the year as Hospital Sunday, so we'll have a Hospital Story from the life of the Saviour. This was one of His great miracles of healing, which He performed while on a visit to Jerusalem. Let us imagine that we were among the onlookers that day at the Pool of Bethesda:—

The Hospital Was Uncomfortable. There were no rows of clean white beds, with devoted nurses in attendance  upon the patients. Instead, there was just a circular building with five porches around the pool, in which lay a mass of crippled, broken humanity. It must have been a cold, depressing place at times, and particularly during the winter, as it offered very little protection from wind and rain. Yet the patients kept waiting on, for an angel visited the pool at irregular times when he troubled the waters and thus afforded a cure to the first person who then stepped into it. Many of them, however, had spent long years there, whose chances of ever being healed in this way were getting less and less. Some of the patients were paralysed, others were blind, or lame; but, whatever their infirmity, each of them wore the same expression of utter hopelessness and despair.

The Patient Was Incurable. When the Lord Jesus
visited this strange place, nobody recognised Him, or even
prayed that He would heal them. He was just an unknown
Stranger to them; yet He knew each patient thoroughly,
and how long they had visited the pool. It seems on this
occasion that He selected the patient who had been there
longest, even thirty-eight years and, in all probability, was the
most hopeless case of all. This poor creature, who had no
friend to help him into the pool at the proper moment, then
met the Best Friend of all. The incurable met the Only One
who could really cure him. The man whose sin had ruined
his life (v. 14) then came face to face with the Son of God who
had come from heaven to put away sin by the sacrifice of
Himself.' As that eventful meeting took place, a new light
must have come into this poor man's eye, for a new hope was
then born in his heart.

The Physician Was Capable. First of all, we observe
His keen interest in the patient. Jesus did not wait until He

was consulted by this helpless man,
but, rather, sought him out where he
was. He was always seeking the poor
and needy that He might bring to
them both physical healing and spiritual blessing. We notice also *His
perfect knowledge of the disease.* In
each case He knew the cause, the
character and the course of the
trouble and how it would end. This
patient's life was like an open book
to Him, for He knew it all. Further,
we see *His loving sympathy towards the needy.* There was
nothing but love in His heart for such, a Divine love, cause-
less, measureless, unmerited, personal and free. Lastly, we
remember *His unbroken record of complete success,* for, in every
case, where He healed the sick, the cure was always perfect—
and required no second visit!

The writer used to spend a few days occasionally with a
well-known Canadian surgeon who was a University lecturer

and a fine Christian. He was never content unless he was doing good to somebody and particularly by means of his medical skill. On one occasion, he recalled the most remarkable year of his career, when he performed many operations; but *only lost one case*, that of a young lad from the country whose parents had delayed too long. What a unique record! And yet, here was One who *never* lost a case.

The Cost was Unbelievable. We never read a word of the sick man being charged anything for this marvellous cure. No bill was presented, no doctor's fees were asked because the Saviour always taught that His cures, like His great salvation, were entirely free. When the Apostle Peter writes about the Cross of Christ he says, "by whose stripes ye were healed" (1 Peter 2. 24). Our healing could only be effected in virtue of His death and, because He completed the whole work of salvation, the cure from the dread disease of sin and its awful consequences comes to us without money or price. Wonderful!

The Cure was Unmistakable (v. 9). Christ's word of command, 'Rise, take up thy bed and walk', brought immediate strength and healing to the patient as he sought to obey. The Lord's wonder-working power was displayed without any excitement, without any effort or struggle; without any waiting, and without charge. The one condition was that of simple faith in the Physician. No wonder, then, that he gladly lifted his mat on which he had lain so long and walked off with it on his back as Jesus had directed. The purpose, no doubt, was to prove to all that the cure was genuine and that he was finished with the pool!

In the days of Henry Moorhouse, the famous English evangelist, there lived a little girl whose parents invited the preacher to be their guest. One evening the child entered his room and exclaimed, "Mr. Moorhouse, I want to be a Christian," so she was asked to read a few verses of Isaiah 53. As she reached the fourth verse, Mr. Moorhouse suggested that she should change the pronouns "we" and "our" into the personal "I" and "my". In this way the girl read on, "'He was wounded for *my* transgressions . . . and with His stripes'"—and here she stopped, while her eyes filled with tears. "Read on, my dear," said Moorhouse, so the little one completed the verse with the word, "*I am healed*'." As she did so she received Christ as her personal Saviour.

The Results were Remarkable. Instead of being congratulated, the healed man was criticised as a law-breaker for daring to carry his bed on the Sabbath! (v. 10). It was nothing less than hatred of the Christ by the Pharisees and other religious leaders; but, of course, they tried to appear sincere, so they sought to make out that Jesus was a law-breaker also, therefore they persecuted Him too. Despite this opposition, however, the Lord met the healed man soon afterwards in order to encourage and assure him. Then He gave him a word of warning *not to return to the old life* and its sinful habits (v. 14). Nobly the young convert obeyed and with great courage, confessed to the people that it was Jesus who had wrought this wonderful cure.

The Great Physician lives today and is still seeking the helpless, sin-sick ones that He might bring to them new life and endless blessing. May we all, like this man, hear His call, trust Him as Saviour, then gladly and courageously take our stand for Him so that others also may seek Him too.

If the healed man had known this well-known chorus he might have been heard singing:—

> *Thank You, Lord, for saving my soul;*
> *Thank You, Lord, for making me whole;*
> *Thank You, Lord, for giving to me*
> *Thy great salvation so rich and free.*

POSTERS

THIS is a day of advertisements, so it is not surprising that we should see so many colourful posters, displayed in prominent places, advertising different products, etc. The following are a selection of these for our interest and instruction:—

The Safety Poster, or *How to Go*. This poster fulfils an important role for it does two jobs in one. It both warns of possible dangers, and also instructs in the laws of safety. The *warning* must be given constantly lest there be any carelessness or neglect. It applies to all who use the roads, drivers and pedestrians alike, and specially to children, lest any unnecessary risks be run, and serious accidents happen. The *instruction*, likewise, must be given repeatedly, so that all may know the way of safety. If we are walking, we must always look both ways before crossing the street. We must also obey the traffic lights, and cross only at the proper places. If there are no traffic lights, however, then we must look for the traffic policeman and trust him to guide us safely over.

This poster may be compared with the Bible, for therein we find the same two things emphasised—warning and instruction. Sin has brought fearful danger; but Christ, by His death and resurrection, has become the way of salvation and life to all who trust Him (John 14. 6).

The Soap Poster, or *How to be Clean*. There is a wide range of posters of this kind from which to choose, all of which seek to advertise that purity and snow-whiteness may be obtained through using one of these products. The fact that there are so many posters of this nature which advertise soaps, washing powders, etc., proves to us that we live in a defiled world, where, with so much smoke, dust and dirt, we may easily become begrimed. And yet, we may never realise this —until we look in the mirror!

A little boy named Alfred came indoors from play, looking very grimy. Teasingly his mother exclaimed, "Go away, you're not my little boy," and the child, almost in tears, replied, "It's me, Mummy, *under the dirt*!" It did not take long, however, to get it all washed away and Alfred was happy again.

Sin, likewise, brings defilement and stains the life, but the glad news of the Gospel tells of perfect cleansing for all who trust the merits of the precious blood of Christ (1 John 1. 7).

The Sleep Poster, or *How to Find Rest*. This poster advertises a product which claims to induce healthful sleep, thus ensuring a good night's rest and freedom from the discomfort of a sleepless night. The secret is simple—Just mix one or two teaspoonsful of this powdered food with hot water and milk, and *drink it*. It is no use just admiring the poster if one wants to enjoy a good sleep! But even then the makers cannot possibly guarantee that it will succeed in every case, seeing that sleeplessness may be caused by many different things—including, perhaps, a guilty conscience! Judging, however, by the large sales of this product and the many testimonials received from satisfied customers, it must give very satisfactory results.

The real secret of rest, however, not only of body, but also of heart and conscience, is only to be found in Him Who said, 'Come unto Me and *I will give you rest*' (Matt. 11. 28).

A little girl lay very ill and could not sleep. Everything possible was done for her, but without success. Then, the exhausted girl put up her hands towards her mother, who knew at once what she wanted. Although forbidden by the doctor to lift her, the mother's love compelled her to act and, with amazing results, for the little one was no sooner in her mother's arms than she fell into a peaceful sleep. From that moment she began to recover because she had found the place of rest. And so may we also find true rest if we pillow our heads on the Saviour's breast.

The Soldier Poster, or *How to Decide*. Here is a young man who cannot make up his mind what career to choose. As he walks down the street, he sees this poster and reads it. He thinks of the special benefits offered, a good training, physically and mentally, his education improved, a trade learned—and he may see the world besides! As he gazes at the picture of a fine, athletic-looking soldier, his mind is made up, and, within a short time, he is on the parade ground, clad in khaki uniform, marching along as a soldier of the Queen.

This striking poster would teach us that if ever we are to be soldiers of the King of kings first of all we must make a definite, personal decision for Christ (John 3. 36). There can be no conscripts in His Army, so the choice, therefore, must be voluntary.

In the days of King David, when he lived in exile, and before he was crowned King of Israel, there came to him men of the tribes of Benjamin and Judah. He did not know whether they were sincere, or merely pretenders; but just then one of their leaders, Amasai, spoke these soul-stirring words: 'Thine are we David, and on thy side, thou son of Jesse' (1 Chron. 12. 18). No wonder David received them into his army. In like manner we must come to the Lord Jesus and take our stand under His royal banner.

It is our happy privilege, also, to wear the King's uniform and display our colours by a public confession of Christ as Lord (Rom. 10. 9). The world is looking on, and we must show them on whose side we are. There is a work to be done, there are orders to be obeyed, enemies to overcome; but, with Christ as Commander, we gladly follow wherever He may lead—and all due to our personal decision for Him.

The Strength Poster, or *How to be Strong*. There are various posters which feature the words *power*, or *strength*, such as electrical power for industry, or physical strength which may be obtained by eating certain advertised foods, etc., or, perhaps, by physical culture. We all desire to be strong and healthy, so we may decide to test the advertisements!

Years ago there used to be displayed two photographs of Sandow, the famous 'Strong Man'. In the first of these portraits he appeared as a weakling, thin and poorly; while in the other picture he looked like a giant, with strong muscles and powerful physique. It was not surprising, then, that this striking advertisement was the means of influencing many young men to adopt his system of physical culture!

It is God's desire that all His children should be strong (Eph. 6. 10), able to stand fast for Him; able to serve Him faithfully; able to play our part nobly for Him. There are conditions, however, before this can be realised:—(1) *We must watch our diet.* We must love the Book and read it constantly for it is the Bread of Life. (2) *We must abstain from anything which would spoil our appetite for heavenly things.* (3) *We must have plenty of exercise,* both indoors and out of doors, for we must both pray and work for the Master. (4) *We must live in the sunshine* as much as possible, just as the eagle loves to soar into the cloudless sunshine of heaven; or, in other words, we must live in the enjoyment of God's love.

There are many other interesting posters, e.g., Savings, Travel, etc., but these may suffice to start us on the heavenward way and keep us marching onward to Glory.

Famous Runners

NEARLY every young person is fond of a good run and more especially if there is a prize for the winner! Sometimes, too, we may see harriers in training, sprinting along the street or, perhaps, doing a cross-country run. There are, likewise, a number of runners mentioned in the Scriptures who, by their running, revealed their character, and thus made possible these interesting Bible stories. In the first case we see a man—

Running for Refuge (Num. 35. 15). In all probability he has been felling a tree and by accident has fatally injured

a fellow-worker. There must be no delay for the brother or other near relative of the dead man will probably seek to avenge his relative's death. There is only one place of safety to which he must run with all speed. It is the nearest of the six Cities of Refuge, three of which are in the country west of the River Jordan, and three others on the eastern side. We can picture him as he races on and on, occasionally looking over his shoulder to see if he is being pursued. If there is no runner in sight, he may rest for a little, now and then; but not for long, for he knows it is, indeed, a race for life. At last, however, he comes within sight of the city, while the people gather along the roadside to watch and cheer him as they recognise that he is *running for refuge*. The gate is then reached and the exhausted runner is kindly received and escorted inside the city to the place of safety, beyond the reach of the avenger.

This Divine provision of long ago still serves as a splendid illustration of God's salvation which is offered to all sinners in the Person of His dear Son. Just as the man-slayer ran for refuge to the city, so each one of us should run to Christ for eternal refuge and salvation. There was no time for delay then, and there is greater need of haste now, so—*run*!

Running to Welcome (Luke 15. 20). At first glance we observe that this runner is not a young man, but a person in middle life, so we know at once that there must be some particular reason for this. We observe that there is a smile on his face for away in the distance, he recognises his long-lost son coming towards him. It is the meeting of the Prodigal son with his father, somewhere between the far country and home, and not, as is usually depicted, just outside the old home. Despite the unpleasant appearance of his wayward boy, the father clasps him to his breast and covers him with kisses. Then they walk home together, rejoicing, for the guilty past is now forgiven and forgotten.

The running father would teach us that *God is in a hurry* to *welcome and forgive* all who turn to Him in repentance. It tells of His wonderful love and His readiness to welcome and forgive the returning sinner.

Running to Tell (2 Sam. 18. 21). After the battle between the forces of King David and his traitor son, Absalom, when the latter was slain, and his army routed, we read of a man named Cushi, who was commanded to run to the King with the glad news of victory. The watchman on the city walls saw him running, and so also did the King, for he was anxious to know the result of the battle. As the runner approached the King he cried, 'Tidings, my lord, the King,' then he proceeded to break the news gently, for Absalom the rebel son had been greatly loved by his father in spite of all his folly. Thus the runner became the news-bearer of a great victory and of a wonderful deliverance from a treacherous enemy.

We, too, may become runners to carry a similar message of victory and deliverance from a far greater enemy, sin, because of the triumph of Christ. The healed Demoniac was told by his Saviour to 'Go home and tell what He had done for him,' and so faithfully did he fulfil his task that the Saviour's fame was spread through all the towns and villages of that district. And thus may we, likewise, *run to tell*.

Running to Make Sure (John 21. 4). This is a chapter of runners for, first of all, we read of Mary running to inform Peter and John that the Saviour's tomb was empty. They, in turn, became runners, too, for they wanted to see it for themselves and thus make sure that Mary's report was true. John was probably the younger man for he won the race and reached the sepulchre first; but Peter was more impulsive than John for he stepped inside the tomb first. There they beheld the grave clothes, just as Jesus had stepped out of them; while the napkin was there, too, folded and laid aside. Mary's story was thus proved to be true and, later in the day, they were to have it confirmed by seeing the risen Saviour Himself. Because the grave is empty and Jesus is risen, then, if we believe in Him, we, too, may be *sure* that all our sins are gone and that we possess life everlasting (1 John 5. 13).

Running to Win (1 Cor. 9. 24). Now for the prize-winning run! Here is an athlete with his eye on the goal. He wears the lightest possible clothing, for any heavy garment would soon hinder his progress. His one ambition is to win the prize, so he strains every muscle to accomplish his heart's desire. There are many difficulties to be overcome, but he keeps on running, until at last he touches the tape—first.

This picture is given to encourage all who have received Christ as Saviour to run well in the Christian race. Let us note some of the secrets of success:—(1) *Runners must train well and exercise self-discipline.* (2) *They must run only on the appointed course.* (3) *They must keep their eyes on the goal* and not on things around or on the other runners. (4) *They must keep up a regular pace* and not just run by fits and starts. (5) *They must reserve sufficient energy to finish the race well* and not allow themselves to gradually weaken towards the end of the race. The Apostle Paul used this illustration frequently and exhorted the believers to run the Christian race with determination and endurance, looking unto Jesus (Heb. 12. 2), the Perfect Pattern.

Coats for All!

THIS strange assortment of coats has a number of interesting stories to tell concerning some Bible characters. It
is a well-known fact that the clothes which one wears often
betray the character of the wearer. It was so at least in the
experience of the people who wore these garments:—

A Special Coat (Gen. 37. 3). This 'coat of many colours'
was given to Joseph by his father, Jacob, as a proof of the
special love which he had for him. It also marked him out
as the father's heir, instead of Reuben, the eldest son, as the
custom was. This is probably the chief reason why Joseph's
brothers envied and hated him. Every time he wore it, it
must have reminded the wearer of his father's love and also
of the many special favours and privileges which went with
it. At the best, however, that parental love was limited and
weak, for it could neither restrain the power of evil, nor rescue
the lad from the cruel plot of his brethren. How different
is God's love which embraces 'whosoever', and knows no
beginning, no change, no weakness, no possible failure,
and will know no end (John 3. 16).

A Stained Coat (Gen. 37. 33). This is
the same coat as the former one—yet not the
same, for it is now stained with big, ugly,
dark marks. On this particular occasion it
was brought home by Joseph's brethren and
shown to their anxious-hearted father who
had worried over the absence of his son
Joseph. In the most heartless manner they
suggested that their brother must have been

torn by some wild beast, when all the time they knew that they had sold him as a slave to the Midianites when they were on their way to Egypt. Thus they deceived their aged father and inflicted upon him a terrible grief which he carried for many years. Thus, they not only told a lie but acted one, too, with the aid of this bloodstained coat.

It is a reminder of Calvary, for what Joseph's brothers did to him, Jesus' brethren, likewise, did to Him when, with cruel treachery, they sold Him for 30 pieces of silver, and ultimately delivered Him to death. Such was the awful hatred of sinful man against the Saviour, which still exists in the hearts of those who refuse Him. This coat with its horrible stains speaks loudly, for it tells of the greatest of all sins, the rejection and death of the Saviour (John 12. 48).

A Steel Coat (1 Sam. 17. 38). Here comes Goliath the giant, in all his boasted strength, laughing at the lad who has dared to accept his challenge to battle. On his body is this heavy coat of shining mail, a sure defence, as he supposes, from every enemy attack. He trusts it to preserve his life, but he is sadly mistaken, for, with one blow in the forehead from David's sling and stone, the mighty champion is laid low in death. Thus through this remarkable victory the enemy is utterly routed and deliverance comes to Israel.

Just as Goliath relied upon his coat of mail to save his life so, likewise, many people trust in something which they can do in order to gain Divine forgiveness and eternal salvation. How foolish this is when God has distinctly declared that salvation is 'not of works, lest any man should boast' (Eph. 2. 8). We must, therefore, discard these things entirely as a means of being saved and rely only in the finished work of Christ.

A Spotless Coat (Matt. 22. 1-13). This lovely white garment is an Eastern wedding robe, which was sent, along with the King's invitation to one of the guests. This person has a special desire to attend the marriage of the King's son;

but he desires to appear in a garment of his own choosing, a rich, colourful robe which will serve to display his personal greatness. Thus, he refuses to wear the wedding garment provided for him, and dares to appear in this robe of his own. When the King comes in to greet the guests he observes this man at once, who presents a striking contrast to all the others who are attired in spotless white garments. Then he aks him, 'Friend, how camest thou in hither, not having on a wedding garment?' and the man is speechless for he knows that he has no reason to give for his folly. Then the King orders his servants to take him away and punish him for daring to treat him with such insolence.

Let us look, also, at the other guests, as they enter the vast hall, where the wedding ceremony is to take place. Each one is dressed in a spotless wedding robe, or coat, provided by the King, for white robes best befit the presence of his majesty.

A number of years ago, when India was under British rule, a major in the army received an invitation to an Indian wedding. As in the Bible story each invitation was given along with the accompanying white garment. But the major, not quite sure of what it meant, never troubled to put it on. When he arrived without it, however, dressed in his best army uniform with flashing medals, etc., and looking resplendent, he was told that he could not be admitted unless he donned the proper garment. Not wanting to miss the wedding he had to "pocket his pride," change his attire, and appear in the provided garment.

This interesting and instructive parable points forward to the wedding of the Lamb in glory (Rev. 19. 7), when all the redeemed will be gathered around the Lord in heaven, all dressed in the spotless robe provided for them by His atoning death. Any garment of self-righteousness will never appear there, but only the spotless wedding robe. That is why we should make sure that we accept the wedding garment now, and thus be made fit for the King's presence by and by.

A Seaman's Coat (John 21. 7). In this last chapter of John's Gospel we see Peter and six other disciples back once more to their former occupation as fishermen on the Sea of Galilee, the place of many happy memories. Peter leads the way as usual, for he was a born leader, and that night they spend on the tossing waves, casting the net in hope of a big catch. Alas, they are disappointed, however, for not one fish is caught after all their toil. As the morning breaks, they steer for the shore, where they see a lone Figure, but know not Who He is. After enquiring of them if they have had any success and hearing of their failure, He commands them to try once more by casting the net on the right side of the ship. It is then that they realise that the Stranger must be none other than the risen Saviour, who had promised to meet them again in Galilee. The order is obeyed, therefore, and, true to His word, the net is filled with shining fish. As the boat approaches the shore Peter wraps his *fisher's coat* about him, plunges into the sea and drags the heavy net behind him. *That is how he meets his Lord by the shore that morning.*

One day we're going to meet Him, too, and He will want to know how many fish we have caught, or, in other words, how many others we have won for Him as 'fishers of men'. The fisher's coat tells of willingness to face much hardship and endure danger, disappointment and difficulty in order to bring others to Himself.

One Saturday evening two boys known to the writer came out of a meeting where they had heard afresh the story of the Saviour's love. It was then decided that they should go for a walk together and, as they did so, the older one asked his friend if he had ever trusted Jesus as his Saviour. That was the beginning of a long conversation which ended happily in the younger boy deciding to receive Him. Then he went home to tell his widowed mother the whole story and, so full of joy was the boy, that he talked about it until nearly midnight! Thus a young fisher landed another fish that night!

Till we meet our Lord on the Golden Strand may we remember His words, 'Cast the net,' and, as fishers of men, toil on in this splendid work of helping others to Him.

The Alarm Box

A S we walk along a city street, we are arrested by the sight of a bright red (or green) coloured object, which stands at the corner. As it is night, we notice that there is a red light on top, flashing every few seconds. As we approach it we see three words prominently displayed on it—**Police, Fire, Ambulance,** so we understand its purpose at once. All that requires to be done in any case of emergency is simply to pull open the door and use the telephone inside as directed so that the Headquarters of the required Service will be informed, and be able to act immediately. Thus the Alarm Box serves a very useful and necessary purpose. Let us look at some of its interesting features.

Fire. Although this is the second word on the Alarm Box, it is the most important word of the three, because fire is the greatest possible danger to life and property. Provision must be made, therefore, to deal with it at once in every town and city. As we think of the character and effects of fire, we think, also, of something which is very similar to it, namely—SIN.

1. *It Starts Easily.* A tiny spark from a passing train has caused great prairie fires. A single match thrown away carelessly has sometimes resulted in the loss of a liner, a train, or much valuable property. Likewise, sin starts very easily. A glance, a thought, a hasty word and the conflagration is begun which may wreck a life and ruin a soul. It was so in Eden's Garden, when Satan dropped the spark of doubt into Eve's mind as he said, 'Hath God

said?' Then he quickly changed God's word from 'ye shall surely die' into 'ye shall *not* surely die.' Thus the fire of sin was started and is still raging worldwide.

2. *It Spreads Rapidly.* The writer spoke with one of the chief men at a city Fire Station and asked him if he could give an instance of this from his own experience. He then related the story of a colossal fire at a chemical works which, he declared, was 'just made to burn.' It went up in flames like an explosion and scattered sparks over a wide area, which started 37 other fires, one of them being a large church about a quarter of a mile away from the original fire.

This fact was also proved repeatedly in the early part of the late war when the Great Fire Blitz of London took place on the 29th December, 1940. The incendiary bombs rained down on many buildings where there were no fire-guards, or too few to cope with them at once. The result was that the flames soon swept from building to building and wrought great destruction; while the firemen could do very little more than prevent it from spreading further. In like manner, sin may spread very quickly and become master, unless it is subdued in time.

3. *It Ruins Permanently.* The grim sight of burned-out buildings makes one tremble at the awful power of fire to destroy precious lives and valuable property. Sin works in a similar manner, also, until, if unchecked, it may ruin both body and soul.

We remember a young lad of about twelve years of age. He had been brought up in London and had come under the influence of a "gang" of boys whose sinful habits were beyond description. This boy came north and very soon influenced a number of others as he himself had been. Then, suddenly, as if by Divine intervention, he was stricken with a serious disease and died.

Some years ago, in the Federal Penitentiary of Leavenworth (U.S.A.) among the prisoners serving sentence were many professional men, including no less than thirty physicians, besides others of high social rank. These were promising lives which had been completely ruined by sin.

Now, let us think of the next word on the Alarm Box:—

Police.   Let us suppose that there has been a burglary in this particular district.   Someone runs to the Alarm Box and informs the police.   Within a few minutes the Police Patrol Van is on the scene then, after an exciting chase, the burglars are caught and escorted to the waiting car.   In this

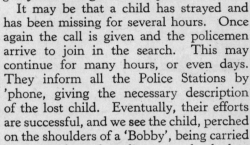

case we see how *the policeman tracks the guilty* and brings them to justice.

It may be that a child has strayed and has been missing for several hours.   Once again the call is given and the policemen arrive to join in the search.   This may continue for many hours, or even days. They inform all the Police Stations by 'phone, giving the necessary description of the lost child.   Eventually, their efforts are successful, and we see the child, perched on the shoulders of a 'Bobby', being carried home!   In this case, we see how *the policeman seeks the lost*.

Perhaps a child may have fallen into a canal or river, and requires to be rescued, but there is no one about who can render this service so, once again, the police are called.   No sooner do they arrive, than we see one of them throwing off his helmet and coat, then diving into the water.   A little later we watch the child being carried out safely, rescued just in time, though it meant rather a cold dip for the rescuer!   In this case, we see how *the policeman rescues the perishing*.

Surely these three instances are illustrations of the work of the Saviour, firstly, by bringing home to the guilty a sense of their sin and its judgment; secondly, we see how He seeks the lost (Luke 19. 10), like the Good Shepherd seeking the lost sheep and, lastly, we observe how He rescues and saves the perishing (John 3. 16).

Then comes our third word—

Ambulance.   This is also an important word for it tells of a very necessary service which is available for anyone who requires to be taken to hospital for immediate medical attention.   Perhaps someone has met with a serious street accident and, knowing there is an Alarm Box nearby, we run along and put through the call to the Ambulance Service. A policeman may be at hand also to render immediate first-aid until the ambulance arrives. We watch the injured person being attended to, then gently carried into the ambulance, which soon moves off. The red cross, prominently displayed on the ambulance reminds us of the Cross of Calvary, where all sin-sick ones may find healing and strength (1 Peter

2. 24). The ambulance team would also suggest the Sunday School teachers and others who seek to bring needy ones to the Great Physician for salvation.

One day four men who lived in, or near, the city of Capernaum heard the wonderful news that Jesus was in the city. They had a very dear friend, or relative, who was paralysed. Now was their greatest opportunity; so, they became an ambulance team, for they made a stretcher and carried their friend to the house where Jesus was. Every moment was precious, as ambulance men know; so, in order to get to Jesus at once, they took off sufficient tiles from the roof and lowered down the sick man.

What a surprise it must have been to everyone! and what a lot of criticism there was from the scribes! But Jesus commended the ambulance team and not only healed the sick man but also forgave his sins (Mark 2. 5).

We may not know much about first-aid, or belong to an ambulance team, but we may all try and bring some sin-sick one to the Saviour like the four good men of Capernaum.

Thus we learn that this little red Alarm Box is a most valuable thing indeed and, we trust, that the lessons drawn from it may result in the salvation of many boys and girls.

The FIRE-ENGINE

IT is a great pleasure to be able to visit a large Fire-Station and be shown the wonders of this most interesting place. If we go with a party, perhaps the Fire Chief will oblige us by putting on a special display for our benefit, just to show us what actually happens when the fire-alarm is given. For our present purpose, however, we'll select the Fire-Engine as our object lesson, and note, in the first place:—

Its Need. If we try to imagine what it would be like in a city which has no Fire-Station, no firemen, and no fire-fighting equipment, we would realise at once the awful danger of living in such a place. The Fire Service, therefore, is most essential if life and property are to be protected. As we inspect one of the large Fire Engines (and Escape) and examine it carefully, it seems to say to us: '*You can't do without me*, for I'm not simply a pretty machine to be polished and

admired, but I am here to do the job of guarding your lives and buildings.'

If the Fire Engine is so necessary, then surely, the Gospel is much more necessary because it provides a far greater protection from a much greater danger than that of fire. We might paint these three words from John 3. 16 on the Fire Engine, SHOULD NOT PERISH, for that is the grand purpose

73

of the sacrifice of Christ. *We all need Him* as Saviour, because of the peril which sin has brought to all mankind, and because of our own helplessness to save ourselves.

Its Cost. A modern Fire Station with all its buildings, equipment and staff costs a very large sum of money to maintain. A Fire-Engine alone may cost from £4,000 and upwards. In Great Britain now it costs nothing for anyone to call out the Fire Brigade as formerly; although the expense must be paid for, partly by the Government and partly by local authorities.

Similarly, salvation is offered without cost to everyone, as a free gift for perishing sinners, because Jesus paid the full price when 'He gave His life a ransom for many' (Matt. 20. 28). The bright red colour of the Fire-Engine also suggests His precious blood, without which there is no salvation (Eph. 1. 7). If our eternal salvation cost Christ so very much in order that He might be able to offer it free to all, then surely we should gladly accept it and thank Him Who paid such a tremendous price.

Its Purpose. The main purpose for which the Fire-Engine has been designed, made and provided is that life and property might be saved. The fireman is taught repeatedly that his first concern should always be to *save life first*, and only after that is done to endeavour to save property.

Likewise, the purpose of the Gospel is to save, not only lives, but also precious souls, from the destructive power of

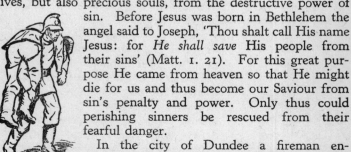

sin. Before Jesus was born in Bethlehem the angel said to Joseph, 'Thou shalt call His name Jesus: for *He shall save* His people from their sins' (Matt. 1. 21). For this great purpose He came from heaven so that He might die for us and thus become our Saviour from sin's penalty and power. Only thus could perishing sinners be rescued from their fearful danger.

In the city of Dundee a fireman endeavoured to reach a blazing room where lay a young child, cut off and apparently without much hope of being rescued. Several attempts were made to reach her, however, but all without success. Then one of the firemen determined to make one last, supreme effort. From the street below, the crowd saw him disappear into the smoke and flame; then, after a few minutes of breathless suspense, they saw him emerge once more, carrying the little one in his arms, and greeted him with a terrific roar of applause. The little girl, though badly burned, survived her fiery ordeal; but her rescuer only lived a few days as he had been burned so severely. His funeral was one of the largest ever seen in the city; for thousands of people lined the main streets as the cortege passed and with bowed heads they paid their last tokens of respect to such a very brave, self-sacrificing man. Thus Christ also gave His life that He might rescue the perishing, save those who were cut off from God and so fulfil His supreme purpose.

Its Power. If this Fire-Engine is to do its job thoroughly, it must have tremendous power. Water may have to be pumped to a great height, through many long hose-lines. The motor engine, too, must be very powerful to be able to stand up to the great strain and carry its heavy load within the shortest time possible.

What is true of the Fire-Engine is certainly true, also, of the Gospel, for we read in Romans 1. 16 that 'it is the *power* of God unto Salvation . . .'; while Hebrews 7. 25 states that 'He is *able* to save to the uttermost . . .'; so we know that His power is all-sufficient for everyone who believes on His name.

Its Speed. The Fire-Engine can do up to 60 miles per hour; while they have the right to dash past the red traffic lights, though the driver must take full responsibility when he does so. The ringing bell gives warning of its approach so that all other traffic may know to give it a clear course to the scene of the fire without any hindrance.

Likewise, the Gospel calls for immediate action, and declares that '*Now* is the day of salvation' (2 Cor. 6. 2). If delay is dangerous with fire, how much more dangerous it is to delay one's decision for Christ. Each time it is put off, it becomes more difficult to decide for Him later, for sin always has a hardening effect. But if one does trust the Saviour in early years the whole life is thus saved from the power of sin with its bitter consequences. We remember that the Lord may come again at any time for His own; so we should make sure that we belong to Him without any further delay.

Its Reach. Some of the escape ladders reach to 100 feet and are usually in three sections which can be run up within a minute or two. Apart from these ladders, rescue work, in many cases, would be almost impossible. Suppose a man is trapped in a room 90 feet up. As he looks down, he thinks, 'I'm beyond the reach of the Escape Ladder,' when all of a sudden he sees it going up and finds to his great joy that it reaches him easily. And what shall we say of the reach of the Gospel? 'For God so loved the *world* . . . *whosoever* . . .' That is the answer, so that no one can say, 'I'm beyond its reach': for no matter how guilty the sinner may be, there is salvation for all.

Its Trustworthiness. Here is another person who is in great danger by fire, a very heavy man, and as he looks at the Escape Ladder, he wonders if it can bear his great weight. Suddenly he hears a fireman shout to him, "Man! *trust* it and get down, or you'll perish," so with fear and trembling he obeys and proves that it bears his weight without any difficulty. And so, also, may every trembling one trust Christ and find that He is the Saviour Who can *always* be trusted.

Its Readiness. It is the boast of firemen that within about two minutes of the alarm being sounded they are on their way, all ready to deal with the fire, for each man is on the job, ready for his task. Likewise, the Lord is 'ready to save' all who call upon Him (Isa. 38. 20). Just as Peter called, 'Lord, save me' when he was going down under the waves of the Lake of Galilee, and was saved immediately by the strong hand of the Saviour, so may all others who call upon Him find that He is ready to save them from perishing.

These are some of the lessons we may learn from the Fire-Engine, which, we trust, may result in a number being 'plucked as brands from the burning.'

THINGS from a BOY'S POCKET

WE'LL imagine that we have found a boy's blazer by the roadside. It looks rather familiar, so we examine it and discover that it belongs to a lad whom we know, for his name is on the tab inside. We carry it home and deliver it to his mother who is very grateful to us and invites us to come inside. After we have a friendly chat, the mother begins to empty the pockets and this is what she finds:—

A Handkerchief. What a colour it is, or rather, *discolour*, for it looks as though it had been used to clean Jack's shoes! No wonder his mother has had to scold him repeatedly for this bad habit, seeing it is almost impossible to wash out all the stains and make it snow-white again. As we look at this spotted and soiled handkerchief we think also of many young lives which have become stained by sin and cannot be cleansed until they are washed and made white in the blood of Christ (Rev. 7. 14).

A Penny. Just a penny! It is the only coin in the pockets, although Jack had been given his usual weekly allowance that morning. It had evidently 'burned a hole in his pocket,' although he had intended to save up for Mother's birthday; but alas, for his good intentions! He was very like the little boy who told his uncle (with obvious intentions!) that he was saving up to buy a £1,000 car, but when asked how much money he had saved, answered, 'Just a penny'! This solitary coin could preach a little sermon and say, 'Just as Jack's money is spent, so everyone is equally poor in the sight of God; in fact, so poor, that they are hopelessly in debt because of their sins.' Although none of us could pay the debt and buy salvation, Jesus, by His death, has paid it all so that we might have it as a gift without having to pay—a penny.

A Magnet. This useful article was bought by Jack and has provided much pleasure and amusement both to himself and also his chums. On these occasions he got a pile of pins, needles, nails, etc., and laid them on the table; then, whenever he placed the magnet near them, they began to jump and dance as if they were alive! The power of electricity in the magnet did the seemingly impossible task of attracting these different articles to itself, besides linking them to each other.

How like the Cross of Christ is the magnet, for Jesus said, 'And I, if I be lifted up from the earth, *will draw all men unto "Me"'* (John 12. 32). The mighty power of His great love attracts and draws us to Himself, and also unites us to everyone who loves Him.

A Knife. This is another of Jack's most useful articles, though it has got him into trouble more than once; as on the occasion when he cut his initials where he shouldn't! It was a birthday present and his name is on it just in case it is lost. With it he has made a number of useful things, including a little boat and an engine. Its two blades are very sharp, in fact, just too sharp, for he has required a little first-aid attention as a result! This knife of many uses reminds us also of the Word of God which is sharper than a sword (Heb. 4. 12) and pierces even to the conscience, when it convicts us of sin. Like Jack's knife, it serves many good purposes. For instance, it cuts the cords of sin which bind us and sets us free, just as Abraham's knife did for his son

Isaac when the ram was found to take his place. As we look by faith to Calvary and see the One Who took our place there, the knife of His Word sets us gloriously free.

A Pen. It is not an expensive one, but a very handy one nevertheless, in fact it was the one used when Jack wrote his last prize essay. Only a very ordinary pen, but what a lot of good work it has done! It resembles all those who, after they have come to the Saviour, have sought to do something for Him. We may not be very talented; but if we place ourselves in the Lord's hand for Him to use, He will write His messages of love and salvation by means of our lives. *The pen must be kept clean*, however, if it is to be used, otherwise there might be blots and ugly splashes to spoil the page. Likewise, we must see that our lives are kept pure and free from sinful habits if we are to be of any use to our Master. *It must be constantly refilled* also and so must we be constantly refilled with His Word, His love, and His grace for that is the kind of ink the King uses!

Abbotsford, the beautiful home of Sir Walter Scott, situated on the River Tweed, contains many very interesting relics associated with the famous novelist. There is his large library with its 20,000 volumes, all bound in leather, also swords, armour, flags, etc. There is also his writing desk, where sometimes he used to start writing soon after 4 a.m. because he was sure of perfect quietness then. There, too, are the quill-pens which he used—not gold ones! They are not much to look at; but, in his hand, see how much they accomplished! And what wonderful things the Lord may accomplish through us, weak instruments though we be, if only we are yielded to Him and ready for His use.

A Magazine. It is a children's magazine which he received at Sunday School and although it is all folded and creased it looks as if it has been well read. This proves to us his interest in the things of Christ, for he seems to have enjoyed reading it. It shows, also, that he likes to read something which helps him to understand and enjoy God's Word. It might have been a 'Penny Horrible' with its crime stories, etc., but instead, it is reading matter which provides encouragement to the young pilgrim on the heavenward way. Surely a good example!

A Badge. This is an attractive badge in red and gold with only two words on it which stand out very boldly—'Jesus Saves.' We wonder why it was in his pocket as we had seen him wearing it regularly. Then we see that the clasp is broken, so it had to go *inside* instead of being displayed *outside*. Sometimes that happens in our experience, too, when, through some circumstance our badge of loyalty is not seen as in former days. In this case, however, Jack was not at fault and will see that he gets a brand new badge next Sunday!

A Mouth-Organ. Jack is very fond of music and is frequently heard whistling as he walks along. He was given this mouth-organ recently by a friend and since then it has been well used and has provided much pleasure. It tells of joy which has come into his life and which he desires to express in tuneful song.

As we look at this unusual array of articles, then, we think of all those people who have been cleansed (the handkerchief), redeemed (the penny), loved (the magnet), freed (the knife), used (the pen), instructed (magazine), and who are loyal (badge), and joyful (mouth-organ), as each of the articles have depicted.

Just then Jack makes his appearance and is both surprised and very much relieved to know that someone has returned his blazer—and also his treasures. After thanking us for this little service rendered, we enjoy a chat together; then, after we part, we still hear strains of music, for Jack and his mouth-organ are not easily parted!

The SHOPS of MAIN STREET

WE'LL suppose that we are visiting a small town, and desire to have a look round the place. After some time, we arrive at Main Street where we commence our tour of inspection of the pricipal shops or stores.

First of all, we come to—**The Newsagent's Shop.** Here we buy a newspaper and read the latest news. It may be summed up as *bad* news, *sad* news, or *glad* news. The bad news may include world unrest, famine, floods, earthquakes, or even war. The *sad* news, very similar to the former, may tell of the death of some outstanding person, or perhaps of an air disaster, or even the passing of a close friend. The *glad* news may describe the deliverance of the nation from some great impending crisis, or perhaps the rescue of the passengers and crew from a doomed liner.

We have important news, likewise, from God's Word— up-to-the-minute and even giving an accurate forecast of future events! The *bad* news tells of unrest because of sin (Isa. 48. 22); the *sad* news tells of death as its wages (Rom. 6. 23); but the *glad* news informs us of the wonderful deliverance of doomed sinners by means of the Gospel (John 3. 16).

Next, we visit—**The Cleaner's Shop,** where we read advertisements which announce that they are able to clean and press any garment, remove any stain, and make it just like new. We hand over a coat to be cleaned and repaired, and the young lady assistant assures us that it will be ready within a day or two.

The lesson we learn here is that our sin-stained garments, likewise, may be cleansed from every spot, so that, through faith in the finished work of Christ, we may stand before God, 'clean every whit' (John 13. 10).

Then we call at—**The Chemist's Shop** (or DRUG STORE). It may be that we want a powder to relieve a headache; or a

tonic which will give us more energy, or perhaps some first-aid dressings. On one of the advertisements displayed inside we see a large red cross, which makes us think of *the* Cross, where there is perfect healing for the sin-sick (1 Peter 2. 24). We note another advertisement also, which displays a certain medicine, with these words printed on it—'Trusted thousands of times.' We notice, too, that there are many people, either handing in a doctor's prescription, or else receiving from the chemist the medicines prescribed. We know that these people cannot read Latin (although a few may know it); neither do they know what medicines the chemist has mixed in the bottles for their different ailments; but *they just take the medicines in good faith*. Here we learn that salvation comes in the same manner, namely, by simple faith. We may not know all the meaning of Calvary; but, as a sick person trusts both the doctor and chemist then takes the medicine, so we, too, may trust the Great Physician and find perfect healing from the dread malady of sin.

Now we come to—**The Milk Shop**. It is probably a warm day, so we desire a refreshing drink. As we look around, we see a number of interesting and colourful posters which tell at a glance the benefits which may be derived from drinking milk regularly. The slogan on each one is 'Drink More Milk,' so we take a glass! Then, there comes to mind 1 Peter 2. 2 which counsels us to earnestly 'desire the sincere milk of the Word, *that ye may grow thereby*.' It is not sufficient merely to know that we have eternal life. The new life must be fed regularly with the best possible food, namely, God's precious

Word, which is both milk to the young believer and also strong meat to the mature Christian, for it contains everything that is essential for our spiritual growth and development.

A little further on we arrive at—**The Gift Shop.** What a lovely store it is! There is every variety of article suitable

 for personal, birthday, or Christmas presents for all ages. There is a large toy department, too, with all kinds of animals, dolls, trains, soldiers, etc., which would delight any child. As we make one or two purchases, we think of God's great gifts which are offered to all, without cost. There are the gifts of forgiveness, peace, eternal life, redemption, joy, satisfaction, power, His precious Word, also the Holy Spirit to dwell within us and, at the end of the road, the gift of heaven itself as our eternal home. Best of all, there is the gift of His beloved Son (John 3. 16); but He must be accepted first before the other gifts can become ours. Such is but a glimpse of the many precious gifts He offers, each one telling us of God's wonderful love.

There is also—**The Music Shop.** Here we find all manner of musical instruments, from the grand piano to the humble mouth-organ! There are also numerous models of wireless and TV sets and, as we examine these, we hear music which is most entrancing coming from another country, jubilant and triumphant. It seems unbelievable, for it comes from such a distant land and makes us think of the heavenly

choirs singing the praises of the Lamb in the Glory Land. No wonder that our hearts are thrilled indeed with such marvellous and inspiring singing. Likewise, we think of the song which is ours now if we belong to Christ, for we, like the Prodigal Son on his return home, have begun to make merry and sing for joy because of the wonderful love which has been lavished on us. Like David we can say, 'He hath put a new song in our mouths' (Psa. 40. 3), and like Billy Bray, we can shout for very joy.

A little boy who had opened his heart to the Saviour, went home to tell his parents of his newly-found joy. The father was a drunkard and threatened to punish him severely if he did not cease singing the Gospel choruses. Time and again the lad had to pull himself up suddenly after letting out one or two notes! One day, however, he was so happy that he forgot all about his father's command and burst out in cheerful song. The angry father stamped his foot and demanded why he had been disobeyed, to which the boy replied, "Daddy, I couldn't help it, for *it just sings itself*!" If we have come to the Saviour, like this lad, we, too, shall be able to sing:

> *I've got the joy, joy, joy, joy,*
> *Down in my heart,*
> *Glory to His Name.*

Lastly, we might mention the **Fruit Shop**. How it attracts boys and girls! They sell fruit which has been grown in different countries and brought to us that we might eat and enjoy them. There are the luscious grapes, the pineapples, the grape fruit, melons, oranges, peaches, plums, apples— and all the others.

Now, if we have become Christians, we are expected to display in our lives what the Bible calls the fruit of the Spirit (Gal. 5. 22). That simply means that we hand over our lives to Christ to dwell in us and take full possession so that His beautiful graces may be seen in us. His love, joy, peace, etc., will then be manifest; while the weeds of self-pleasing will be kept out.

And what a lovely world it could be if we all did that!

The WONDERS of NIAGARA FALLS

(A Lesson for Older Children)

WE purpose taking an imaginary trip to these famous falls and, as we view them in all their beauty and splendour, we'll seek to use them as a giant object lesson in order to teach some helpful lessons.

Niagara Falls were discovered in 1678 and are still regarded as one of the wonders of the world. Below Grand Island, the Niagara River plunges forward in rapids till it reaches the part where, split by Goat Island, half a mile of water pours over in sheets of thousands of tons. The American Fall is 1,060 feet wide, with a fall of 167 feet. The Canadian, or Horseshoe Fall, with its majestic inward curve of 3,010 feet and a sheet of water 20 feet in thickness, takes a plunge of 158 feet. The mass of water leaps so far forward that it is possible to pass underneath into a misty cave, curtained by foam and spray. There one sees many beautiful rainbows, some four or five yards in span, leaping from rock to rock. The river then rushes through a narrow gorge, taking a sharp turn to the left, where it forms the famous Whirlpool, and finally flows on until it enters Lake Ontario.

Let us now compare and contrast some of the wonders of Niagara with the greater wonders of Calvary:—

A Wonderful Work. When we look at the Falls, we realise that they are nothing less than the handiwork of God, the Creator, and not the product of man's genius, for he had no part whatsoever in this great work. It is not surprising, therefore, that, as people gaze at this wonderful display of Divine power and wisdom, they are filled with a sense of awe and are lost for words to describe its beauty.

As we think of Calvary we are compelled likewise to confess, 'This is the work of God,' for no mere man could ever have accomplished the mighty miracle of salvation as Christ did there (John 19. 30). We know that that great work was very *costly* for He had to give Himself, *perfect* because He died in our stead, and *sufficient* because it avails for all. The more we think of Calvary, the more the wonder grows upon us that He should even love us so much as to give Himself for us.

We remember the first time we visited Niagara Falls. We had heard of some people who lived within easy distance of reaching there, but had never done so, though they had always promised they would. Then when we walked over the Bridge and stood gazing at the spectacle of dazzling beauty, a sense of awe overcame us. We were speechless. The whole scene of unique glory so filled us with a sense of our littleness and God's greatness that we could only wonder and worship!

A Wonderful Attraction. From nearly every country of the world people come to visit Niagara Falls, drawn thither by its beauty and charm. Whether it be in summer, with all its warmth and sunshine, or in the autumn, with all its golden colours of glory and beauty, or during the winter months when everything is wrapped in a dazzling mantle of snow and ice, it's appeal is always irresistible. The powerful, coloured lights which shine on the Falls from the Canadian side enhance the beauty still more, and present a wonderful appearance of dazzling glory.

As we think, also of Calvary, we know that people of many nations have been drawn thither, and are still being drawn by its wonderful appeal. When anticipating the Cross, the Lord Jesus declared: 'And I, if I be lifted up from the earth, *will draw all men unto Me'* (John 12. 32). Because of His amazing love for all mankind, He was willing to suffer such a death that many might be drawn to Himself for salvation. Is it any wonder, then, that His great love should draw us to Himself and make Him become to us the supreme attraction?

A Wonderful Blessing. After we have spent some time viewing the famous Falls, we make our way to one of the giant power stations close by. We learn that a great wall is built into the river to divert part of the water to what is called the forebay. From here the water passes into the penstock, the huge pipe through which it falls 180 feet with terrific force, turning the turbines at the bottom. The turbines, in their turn, revolve the generator which generates the electricity. The current is then carried by wires to the distributing station above and sent from there to light cities and work the machinery of great factories over a wide area. Because of this endless stream of power, the wheels of industry are kept revolving and the pay packets of the workers are assured.

Let us suppose, however, that because of some great, unforeseen catastrophe, Niagara fails! What darkness there would be in homes, streets and factories, and what suffering it would bring to very many people of both Canada and U.S.A. Fortunately, there is no likelihood of such a calamity ever happening.

Calvary, too, is the source of an endless stream of blessing to mankind. Like Niagara, light streams from this sacred spot which, as the Gospel is proclaimed, may lighten the darkest corners of the heathen world. Unlimited power is also available here, far greater than that provided by the harnessing of Niagara Falls; for it is sufficient to meet the needs of all mankind, both for time and eternity. It is a *cleansing* power, an *enabling* power, a *transforming* power, a *controlling* power, the inexhaustible power of God (1 Cor. 1. 18).

A Wonderful Position. Niagara Falls occupies a unique position, being situated on the border between U.S.A. and Canada. Calvary, also, is on the border—not between two countries, but, rather, between two attitudes of mind and heart, namely, faith or unbelief. Calvary divides all mankind into these two groups—either those who believe on Christ as their Saviour, or those who do not believe on Him (John 3. 36). These two classes were represented by the two thieves who were crucified on either side of Jesus, one of whom believed on Him and boldly declared his faith; while the other man refused to believe on Him or accept Him. Calvary occupies this unique and central place, therefore, where everyone must make their choice, either for Him or against Him—a choice upon which rests their eternal destiny.

Some years ago a young couple visited the Falls at the end of winter and crossed the famous Ice-Bridge. As they did so, however, a sharp sound was heard, like a rifle shot. *It was the first crack in the bridge*, due to the thaw. Immediately the girl was seized with a terrible fear, so the young man waited a little while until she calmed down, then sought repeatedly to coax her to step over the crack on to the safe side. All his efforts were unsuccessful, however, and the gap began to widen quickly. The young man was finally compelled to jump back for the last time; while, with a breaking heart, he watched his sweetheart being carried away on the broken Ice-Bridge to a fearful death—and all because she did not act in time.

These are just a few of the wonders of Niagara Falls, viewed in the light of the greater wonders of Calvary, which, we trust, may draw many to Himself. Thus we in turn may become wonders, too, of His grace, through whom His light may shine and His power be manifested as we seek to serve Him in this dark world of sin.

A Wonderful Tree

THE Christmas Tree is supposed to have been derived from the custom of the ancient Egyptians, who used to deck their houses at this period of the year with branches of date-palm, their symbol of life triumphing over death. The Romans introduced it into their country and later into Germany, from whence the custom spread over a large part of Europe. The Christmas Tree was very little known in England before the coming of Prince Albert, the husband of Queen Victoria, who introduced the custom from Germany. To-day, the Christmas Tree plays a very important part in the Christmas celebrations and affords great pleasure, particularly to children. Vested in raiment of tinsel, this glittering chandelier of evergreen and silver, topped by a spangled star and a score of coloured lights, becomes the gathering centre of the family and the treasure trove of many lovely gifts.

The name Christmas reminds us particularly of Christ, whose coming into the world as the Babe

of Bethlehem it celebrates. But it also declares that the holy
Babe Jesus was, in due time, to die on Calvary's Tree so that
He might save His people from their sins (Matt. 1. 21). Thus
we note a number of striking similarities and contrasts between the Christmas Tree and that rugged Cross, the Tree
on which the Saviour died:—

It is a Special Tree. The Christmas Tree is entirely
different from all other trees. (1) It is the only Tree which is
entirely connected with Christmas and with Christ. (2) It
affords more joy to children the world over than any other
tree. (3) On its branches are a variety of lovely gifts, fruit
which is only gathered on this Tree. When we think of His
Cross, we remember that it was a *special* Tree, because here
only can the peoples of the world find salvation, joy and an
abundance of gifts which prove to us God's wondrous love.

It is a Necessary Tree. The Christmas Tree has become
to many people an essential part of the Christmas celebrations
and without it there would be a great lack. All young people
who have been accustomed to have a Tree certainly want to
have it each succeeding Christmas.

In a certain home in Britain during the dark days of the late
war, preparations were being made for Christmas, but without a Tree, as they were so scarce then and very expensive.

The youngest member of the family, however, decided to
take the matter into his own hands, for he felt that a Tree
had to be procured without fail. Thus he set off on his own
with wheelbarrow and axe. As he lived in a small town it did
not take him long to get into the country, where he foraged
around until he found a large branch of a fir tree, which
served the purpose splendidly—and thus saved the situation!

There may be some who do not regard the Christmas
Tree as really necessary; but when we think of Calvary's Tree
everyone must confess that *it was most essential* if sinners
were to be saved. If Christ had not died on the accursed
Tree, there would have been no hope of salvation for anyone;
but because He suffered there all who believe on Him may
know their sins forgiven and enjoy eternal life, with countless
blessings besides.

It is a Suffering Tree. The bright axe blade flashes as the forester, with a few swift blows, fells the Christmas Tree. This little tree of the forest, with its green spire pointing to the sky and its evergreen leaves, the sign of endless life, *because it has died,* is now devoted to a new purpose entirely.

The Christmas Tree thus teaches the important truth of *substitution.* Because it gives up its life it is able, therefore, to bring joy and blessing to many. And because Jesus took our place on the Tree of shame, and died for us, we may rejoice in His great salvation.

During the fighting in the Far East between the American forces and the Japanese troops in the Second World War, an American private named Richard Anderson dropped a grenade accidentally. When he saw it rolling towards his comrades, he threw himself on it and was killed instantly; but in performing this heroic act he saved their lives. Likewise, the Saviour came between us and eternal death when He gave His life for us that we might enjoy eternal salvation.

It is an Attractive Tree. Martin Luther, the great reformer, is said to be the person who first put a few candles on a little pine tree and called his family into the nursery to admire the spectacle. Since that modest demonstration, the Christmas Tree has become illuminated with various lights which make it most attractive and show that Jesus, the Light of the world, has come.

There is the *blue* light, which reminds us of heaven, from whence He came in order that He might bring us there at last, to be with Himself in His eternal home. The *white* light suggests also His perfect sinless life, and also the purity enjoyed by all who are cleansed from their sins. The *red* light tells of the price He paid for our redemption, His precious blood. There is the *green* light, too, which gives the thought of life. The *yellow* light reminds us also that when Christ enters the life there is *joy.* The *orange* light indicates that Christ is now the exalted Saviour, for it is the *glory* colour; while it points forward, also, to His coming again. Thus each flashing light reveals something of Him who is the Light of the world (John 8. 12) and attracts many lost ones to

Himself from the darkness of sin. Perhaps the star on top is illuminated also and this would suggest the star which attracted the Wise Men of the East and led them to Jesus.

It is an Enriching Tree. Hidden in its branches and around its base are many treasures, presents and packages, all waiting to be claimed on Christmas morning. It is not surprising, therefore, that children often find it difficult to go to sleep on Christmas Eve!

It was Christmas morning. The bedroom clock had just struck three and, as it did so, a little boy wakened up, rubbed his sleepy eyes and jumped out of bed. After rousing his sister, they both tip-toed downstairs to see what presents there were for them on the Christmas Tree. Fortunately, a large fire had been kept burning in this room until a late hour, so it was still warm when the children collected their presents, then sat down to open them, while, meantime, they ate some fruit and sweets. Not until everything had been duly inspected and admired did they retrace their steps to bed, carrying with them their treasures, while Daddy and Mummy knew nothing of their exploit until breakfast time!

At the Cross of Christ, too, we gather rich treasure, gifts which prove to us God's great love and remind us of the price

paid by the Saviour in order that they might come to us free. These are gifts which cannot fade or change, for they are eternal. As we gaze at 'the wondrous Cross on which the Prince of Glory died,' we see around it this vast array of marvellous gifts. There is forgiveness of sins, salvation in all its fulness, eternal life, etc., for the gifts are too numerous to mention. But merely looking at them will never make them our own. We must accept them with grateful hearts and give Him our thanksgivings. Then, like the Wise Men of old, we should fall at His feet and worship Him for all His wonderful love, His priceless gifts and above everything else, for *Himself*, God's Gift (2 Cor. 9. 15).

A Ruck-Sack

THE ruck-sack suggests to us that we are on a journey—the journey of life—and, of course, are travelling to a desired destination. While we travel along, however, we require certain articles which will be of great service to us, so let us look over some of them:—

First of all, we must have a **Map** so that we can see just where we are, the danger spots we must avoid and the route along which we hope to travel. Our map is the Bible, the only reliable guide map, for from it alone we learn exactly where we are, namely, in the City of Destruction, like Pilgrim in Bunyan's famous allegory. But it shows us, also, the way we ought to take, the only way of Salvation and blessing, which begins at the Cross, where we lose the burden of sin and thence travel on the King's Highway, upward, onward and homeward to the Celestial City. How very necessary it is, then, that we possess this valuable map.

Next comes a **Pillow**. It speaks of *rest* for that is what we receive whenever we lose our sin-burden. How unlike poor Jacob with his guilty conscience who, after cheating and robbing his brother, fled for his life and when he lay down to sleep had a stone for a pillow. Matthew 11. 28 tells us how this rest may be procured, namely, by our coming to Him; then each day, as we share the yoke with Him, we learn further the secrets of His rest. Having this great blessing we'll be well able for the uphill path, even though it may lead at times to the Hill Difficulty.

We must have a **Blanket**, also, for we are sure to meet with cold winds as we climb to higher heights. Without it we would surely perish; therefore we see that it is one of the first articles placed in the ruck-sack. Whenever we look at it, we think of *warmth* and protection and that in turn reminds us of the warmth of God's wonderful love and of the words of John 3. 16—'For God so loved the world . . . should not perish . . .'

When an American Indian heard the story of God's matchless love from a missionary in an Indian settlement he was so affected by the message that he rose and laid at the feet of the missionary his most treasured possessions—his tomahawk, bow and arrows and several other articles including his *blanket*. He was saying, in effect, if Christ should love me so much, then I want to show my love for Him in return.

A **Mirror**, likewise, is a very essential thing to carry in our ruck-sack just to show what we look like. It is rather unpleasant when we discover that we have been going all the day with some dirty marks on the face when, if we had just taken time to look in the mirror all would have been so different!

The Bible is sometimes likened to a mirror as James 1. 23, 25 tells us, because it shows us what we really are, not merely on the outside, but also in the inside!

Sometimes people have been known to smash a mirror when they see themselves untidy and unclean. The writer saw a huge mirror which had been smashed by a man under the influence of drink. The sight was too much for him!

How much more sensible it is to thank God for showing us our sinfulness and seek the cleansing He gives as seen in our next article.

A cake of **Soap** also must be included in the kit of the pilgrim if the traveller is to be clean. Otherwise he would soon become grimy and travel-stained. Psalm 119. 9 both asks a question and answers it: 'Wherewithal shall a young man cleanse his way? by taking heed thereto according to thy Word.' That is splendid advice for the young pilgrim for the regular reading of the Scriptures keeps him clean. It cleanses the mind from evil thoughts, the mouth from evil words and the life from evil habits, just as water washes away defilement. But we must remember it is not sufficient to possess the soap—we must *apply* it!

Here, also, is a **Dutch Water Bottle**, a very necessary article indeed, specially when the traveller has been tramping or climbing for some considerable time where there is no water available to quench one's thirst.

Perhaps you will remember one of the early journeys of David Livingstone when he had with him his wife and children. Day after day passed and they saw no sign of water. How piteously the boy and girl appealed for it and the self-sacrificing father denied himself and poured out the last drop they possessed to slake their burning thirst. Then, after three days without water, their prayers were answered.

The water-bottle would suggest to us the thought of satisfaction, such as that which came to the Samaritan woman who came for water and instead received a well within! No wonder she went forth telling everyone of her joy for she had experienced that Jesus satisfied her every longing.

Don't let us forget the **Hold-All**, also. There are two kinds, namely, that which holds knife, fork, spoon, etc., or it may be the smaller kind for holding needles, thread, buttons, etc.

When the Children of Israel journeyed for forty years across the desert to the Promised Land, a remarkable miracle was wrought on their garments and footwear for they never wore out! They required no hold-alls! Not so with us, however, for we must attend to our garments and apply the needle from time to time so that we may look our best and not like a tramp with tattered clothes!

The Bible tells us of several outstanding personalities who used the needle to good account, particularly Dorcas, who made garments for the poor (Acts 9. 36); while the great Apostle Paul must have employed it often when he used his craft as tent-maker in order to help pay expenses and thus pursue his missionary work. Let us see to it, then, that we use the needle regularly and so preserve our pilgrim garments intact.

The **Log-Book** must not be omitted either, for we desire to keep a record of our doings on the way, just as every captain keeps a log-book of his ship's movements. If we don't make much progress on our journey, then the log-book will reveal it; but, if we go on well, the progress will be seen at once in this record. How interesting it is to keep a diary, specially if it is read some years later! Then we can recall some of the blunders we made and how we learned by our failures. Well, the log-book is a sort of diary in which we record God's faithfulness day by day and also our various doings. May we be able to write in it what Columbus wrote in his log-book when his wild, rebellious sailors threatened to throw him into the sea because there was still no sign of land ahead. His words were: 'We sailed on'! and so should we, with a similar determination, go on until the goal is reached.

There are a number of other things which we want to pack into the ruck-sack, but these no doubt may prove sufficient for our present purpose. The main thing is to see that we have the Guide with us, then all will be well.

Printed at the Press of the Publishers